THE STRUGGLE
FOR BRAZIL

Portugal and
"The French Interlopers"
(1500–1550)

REGINA JOHNSON TOMLINSON

THE STRUGGLE FOR BRAZIL

Portugal and "The French Interlopers"

(1500–1550)

LAS AMERICAS PUBLISHING CO.
152 East 23rd Street
New York, N.Y. 10010

For my husband Jack
and
To all voyagers

CONTENTS

CHAPTER I

EXCLUSIVE RIGHTS

When Christopher Columbus returned from his 1492 voyage in search of Cathay, there was considerable speculation on where he had been. It began before he even reached Spain or had communication with the Catholic monarchs. En route to Palos a storm blew his sails to shreds and he was forced to enter Lisbon harbor. In a message to the King of Portugal he reported that he had just sailed "not from Guinea, but from the Indies." John II doubted it. He thought it more likely that Columbus had been in southern waters granted to Portugal.[1]

Columbus had not attempted to reach Guinea, but even so the Portuguese had reason for concern. Ever since they had pioneered down the coast of West Africa, they had been plagued by trespassers. Attempts to suppress information about voyages and profits had not been successful. Before long, traders from Seville, Cadiz, Palos and San Lucar heard about the business opportunities in Guinea and ships were outfitted to sail there.

John II's father, Afonso V, had also brooded about interlopers. He felt that Portugal had legitimate claims to Guinea and that others could be excluded. His subjects had been the first Christians to reach that far down the coast, and, according to some observers, the Holy

Father had granted to the Kingdom of Portugal all the land discovered between Cape Bojador and the Indies. The agitation which the interlopers were causing presented an excellent opportunity to advance Portugal's claims.[2]

Don Afonso made some suggestions to Rome. The result was the papal bull ROMANUS PONTIFEX issued by Nicolas V in 1455. After remarking that Portuguese envoys had no part in initiating or composing it, the bull read:

> ... the right of conquest which in the course of these letters we declare to be extended from the capes of Bojador and of Não, as far as through Guinea, and beyond toward that southern shore, has belonged and pertained, and forever of right belongs and pertains to the said King Afonso, his successors, and the Infante, and not to any others.[3]

Rome had spoken but it exercised no control over men at sea or their hunger for trade. The disputing in the Atlantic islands and on the African coast continued. War at home soon took to the sea. During the 1475-79 conflict over the throne of Castile, the Portuguese teamed with the anti-Castile element in the Canary Islands. In return the Castilians openly sent ships to Guinea. The resulting Treaty of Alcaçovas attempted to resolve some of the overseas disputes. Castile was not to molest the Portuguese monarchs "in their present or future possession or quasi-possession in all the trade, lands, and barter in Guinea" or in any of the Portuguese islands from the Canaries to Guinea. The Castilians gained the Canaries. The penalty for violation of the treaty was 300,000 gold doblas.[4]

The treaty was no more successful than the bull had been. Actually, it stimulated the business of interloping.

In came ships from other parts of Spain, France, England and the Lowlands. Merchants in Genoa, Florence, Flanders and England purchased and marketed the cargo. Portugal needed a stronger guarantee.[5]

Again, Rome spoke. Again, the words were favorable to Portugal. A bull issued in 1481 more or less repeated, and thus sanctioned the Treaty of Alcaçovas. The Portuguese were pushing south. In 1483 Diogo Cão reached the mouth of the Congo River. But now Spain too was undertaking long voyages. When Columbus returned from his voyage to the west, Ferdinand and Isabella notified the Vatican at once. They appealed to their Valencian friend, Pope Alexander VI, for official privileges.[6]

Four bulls were issued from Rome. The first, *Inter Caetera*, dated May 3, 1493, took nothing away from Portugal. It declared that Castile would now have the same right to discover, claim, and rule. Any land not already possessed by a Christian prince was fair ground. *Eximiae Devotionis*, issued the same day, states the same thing in more precise language. A second *Inter Caetera* dated the following day, returned to a geographical division of the globe, rather than a simple race to find unclaimed places. The bull declared that Castile and Leon could not only claim unpossessed lands, discovered by her envoys, but also, "all the dominions, cities, camps, places and villages, and all rights . . . all islands and mainlands found and to be found, discovered and to be discovered, towards the west and south . . . (of) a line from the Arctic Pole . . . to the Antarctic Pole . . . one hundred leagues towards the west and south . . . (of) the Azores and Cape Verde."[7] This broad description did not cede land already possessed by 1493. All outsiders regardless of rank or power were forbidden to enter the area granted to the Spanish monarchs without their permission. The penalty was automatic excommunication.[8]

John II could not accept the bull. All it said was that Spain could not claim any possessed land which lay west of the line. He was not certain where Columbus had been, and he was anxious to establish exclusive fishing rights for the Portuguese south of Cape Bojador. Previous bulls had granted that region even "as far as to the Indians" to Portugal.[9] John II prepared a fleet to sail to Columbus' land. The Spaniards were again consulting with Rome and emerged with the bull *Dudem Siquidem,* September 26, 1493. Spain was to gain any lands she should find sailing to the west or south "whether they be in western parts or in the regions of the south and east of India." It voided earlier implications that land in a certain area might belong to someone else.

John II's fact-finding expedition was ready to sail. He also sent an envoy to the Spanish monarchs. They were not opposed to negotiations as it was the Portuguese not the pope who threatened their overseas possessions. It was agreed that Spain would keep clear of the traditionally recognized Portuguese possessions (the Canaries to Guinea area) but that Portugal was not to go into Spain's new land. The Portuguese still were not certain where that was. More ambassadors were sent, and more meetings were held. The Portuguese argued that the arbitrary line dividing the Spanish world from the rest of the globe was too close to the Cape Verde Islands, and Portuguese territory. They suggested that it be moved west and placed closer to the land Columbus said he had found. On June 7, 1494, The Treaty of Tordesillas was signed. The Line of Demarcation was removed from 100 to 370 leagues west of the Cape Verde Islands. Lands east of that line were to be Portuguese, west of it Spanish.

Anything found on the wrong side of the line had to be relinquished to the rightful owner. Except for Spanish ships passing through Portuguese waters to reach west of the line, there was to be no trespassing. No other nation was included or invited.[10]

Spain and Portugal had negotiated and signed a private agreement. Those who had not signed it did not respect it. They were not impressed by the papal authority. The pope claimed the power to decree ownership of newly discovered lands on the grounds that he was Christ's representative on earth and the spiritual father of the world. The excluded merchants and sailors argued that in the 14th century the Venetians had traded with the Saracens against the pope's wishes, and that in the 15th century the popes had weakened their powers of arbitration by taking sides in Italian squabbles. Above all, they could not believe that the pope's declarations demanded respect if two monarchs had taken it upon themselves to have moved the Line of Demarcation without even consulting the pope.[11]

Among those who would not have their sailing routes dictated by anyone were the French. Theirs was a small fleet and they had not been the first in Africa, but they had been engaged in piracy and commerce for many years. Trade by sea had become more important to them every year.[12] There are records of great strides in merchant shipping taken by Normans in the 12th and 13th centuries, and of the arming of ships in the 13th and 14th centuries. The French were the first Europeans to claim the Canary Islands. They, like the Spanish and Portuguese, had obtained rights from the pope, but no special prerogatives had been granted.[13]

Since the beginning of the 13th century, some Frenchmen had considered piracy a profession of "great honor" and there was pride in the title "Duc des Pirates." Sometimes courts of law sanctioned piracy. At times " . . . Norman commerce had the physiognomy of a small war."[14]

But piracy required secrecy. The legal owners of the divided globe looked upon any intruders as criminals and treated them accordingly.[15] Safety entailed more than avoiding capture at sea. Portuguese agents were planted in French ports to seek information on interlopers and to copy the charts of departing ships.[16]

Had the French crown been more interested in trade in the west, it might have established some description of policy for the aid and protection of mariners. But the court's interests were on the continent and to the east. Measures for protection as well as financing, management and equipment of voyages were of local origin.[17]

NOTES

1) J. W. Blake, *European Beginnings in West Africa, 1454-1578. A Survey of the first century of white enterprise in West Africa, with special emphasis upon the rivalry of the great powers.* (London: Longmans, Green, 1937), p. 67.

   S. E. Morison, *Portuguese Voyages to America in the Fifteenth Century.* (Cambridge: Harvard University Press, 1940), p. 83. Professor Morison cites the Court Chronicler's Record of John II's thoughts on the Columbus voyage in *Cronicas d'el Rey João II in Coleção de Livres Ineditos da Historia Portuguesa.* ed. J. Correa da Serra (Lisboa: 1792), II, p. 178.

   S. E. Morison, *Admiral of the Ocean Sea.* (Boston: Little Brown, 1942), pp. 340-344.

2) Blake, *European Beginnings,* pp. 17-20, 66. Blake cites Ruy da Pina, *Cronica del Rey D. Affonso V,* ch. cxlv. The papal grant to which Afonso and others referred was supposedly issued between the years 1417 and 1431 by Martin V. This bull has never been found and perhaps never existed.

3) Frances G. Davenport, *European Treaties Bearing on the History of the United States and its dependencies to 1648.* (Washington D. C.: Carnegie Institution, 1917), pp. 13-26.

Blake, *European Beginnings,* pp. 21-22.

4) Davenport, *European Treaties,* pp. 44-45.

5) Blake, *European Beginnings,* p. 57.

6) Blake, *European Beginnings,* pp. 67-68.

7) Davenport, *European Treaties,* pp. 64-67.

8) Davenport, *European Treaties,* p. 77.

9) Davenport, *European Treaties,* p. 31. The quote is from *Inter Caetera,* March 13, 1456.

10) André Julien, *Les Voyages de Découverte et les premiers éta- blissements (XV-XVI siècles),* Colonies et Empires, ser. 3, no. 1. (Paris: Presses Universitaires, 1948), p 32.

Blake, *European Beginnings,* p. 68.

Davenport,*European Treaties,* pp. 84-85, 95, 107-111. Moving the Line of Demarcation west placed the shoulder of Brazil on the eastern side of it. Now Portugal would seek sanction of the new location of the Line of Demarcation as defined in the Treaty of Tordesillas. In 1506 three bulls were issued confirming the treaty.

11) Blake, *European Beginnings,* pp. 68-71.

Julien, *Les Voyages de découverte,* p. 32.

12) Julien, *Les Voyages de découverte,* pp. 1-14.

13) Edouard H. Gosselin, *Documents authentiques et inédits pour servir à l'histoire de la marine normande et du commerce Rouen- nais pendent les XVIe et XVIIe siècles.* (Rouen: Imprimerie de Henri Boissel, 1876), pp. 3-5.

Julien, *Voyages de découverte,* p. 5. Jean de Béthancourt and Gadifer de la Salle sailed to the Canaries in 1392 and 1402, and obtained privileges from the pope.

14) Gosselin, *Documents,* p. 7.

Ernest Fréville de Lorme, *Mémoire sur le Commerce Maritime de Rouen depuis les temps les plus reculés jusqu'à la fin du XVIe siècle,* I. (Paris: Chez Auguste Durant, 1857), p. 337.

15) Paul Gaffarel, *Histoire du Brésil Français au seizième siècle.* (Paris: Maisonneuve, 1878), pp. 19-20, 90.

16) Charles de la Roncière, *Histoire de la Marine Française,* III. (Paris: Librairie Plon, 1906), p. 267.

17) la Roncière, *Marine Française,* p. 243.

Ernest Lavisse, *Histoire de France depuis les origines jusqu'à la révolution,* I, part I. (Paris: Hachette, 1911), p. 278.

CHAPTER II

THE ROUTES

There were thirteen ships. The destination was India. Under the command of Pedrálvares Cabral, the expedition set out from Belem, Portugal on Monday, March 9, 1500. On board were two mariners of extraordinary experience.[1] One was Bartolomeu Dias, the captain of the first modern fleet to round the Cape of Storms, later renamed the Cape of Good Hope by King John II who indeed hoped that India was not far from the tip of Africa.[2] The other was Nicolau Coelho, a former commander of one of Vasco da Gama's caravels, negotiator with monarchs of the Orient, navigator of great repute.[3]

In *caravelas, navios* and *naus,* the mariners sailed out of the River Tejo. Running before the North-East trade wind, they first reached the Canary Islands, where they were becalmed for a day, then again got under way. On March 22, they sighted St. Nicholas's Island in the Cape Verde Islands. Thence, according to Pedro Vaz de Caminha, the ships "continued on our way across the ocean . . . until on . . . April 21, we came across some signs of being near land, at some 660 or 670 leagues from the aforesaid island, by the pilot's computation."[4] That statement reveals almost nothing about the route. More can be learned from examining the Atlantic winds, past and present sailing instructions, and commentaries on other expeditions.

The ships of Pedrálvares Cabral's day could not sail as close to the wind as can today's sailing ships. From that day to this, much has been learned about basic design. The little Portuguese fleet was made up of two major types of design: the square-rigger, large and easy to manage with a relatively small crew, and the triangular sailed lateen rigged ship. The lateen type was usually smaller and performed better close to the wind, but it needed a large crew to deal with the weighty spars.[5]

After mariners discovered where the high roads of the sea were, they took their ships miles away from the obvious direct routes to use them. Then and now, vessels setting out from Europe for the Cape of Good Hope first sailed south to the Cape Verde Islands, then shaped a course to the southwest. The course varies with the time of year. Present day instructions from the British Admiralty advise that the mariner cross the equator well west of the Cape Verde Islands to steer clear of the doldrums. When south of the equator the ship should "stand across the Southeast Trade on the port tack, even should the vessel fall off to W. by S." as the wind will become more easterly until it is finally an East wind. The ship will then be at the western limit of the Southeast Trade wind. It will also be well out to sea, perhaps not far from Brazil. The mariner is warned to watch for the St. Paul Rocks and Fernando Noronha Island. For most of the year the Southeast Trade wind fails on a line drawn from the Martin Vaz and Trindade Island to the Cape of Good Hope. Upon reaching this imaginary line, the mariner reaches new winds blowing roughly from West to West Southwest. The ship can now be put about and run or reach on a southeasterly course toward the Cape of Good Hope.[6]

The high road to the tip of Africa was discovered only after many years of trial and disappointment. Bartolomeu Dias probably did not strike out to sea but stayed close to the shore. This had been the way Portuguese mariners had first inched their way down the coast of West Africa. Upon reaching Angra das Voltas, some 550 miles north of the tip of Africa, Dias had turned seaward. Whether he intentionally stood off the coast to allow himself searoom to proceed south or simply was blown westward is unknown. Without even realizing it at the time, he cleared the cape. In *Primeira Década da Asia,* João de Barros wrote that Dias "ran for thirteen days with the sails hoisted half way up the mast, when the wind lessening, they sought the land, which hitherto in general had been north and south." When the land completely disappeared, Dias turned north and again found it. He had doubled the tip of Africa, Cape Agulhas. He continued east but a near mutiny forced him to turn back. While homeward bound he actually saw the Cape of Good Hope.

The point where Dias turned back for Portugal was near a river. The captain of Dias' second ship, San Panteleam, Joam Infante, had been the first ashore and had apparently named the river. It was called do Infante.[7] This mariner is surrounded by confusion for he appears in an earlier expedition to the south or perhaps it is another version of the same voyage. It was recorded by a secretary to Afonso d'Albuquerque, Gaspar Correa. He was not the most reliable of historians. Correa said that King John II outfitted four caravels for a foreign merchant named Janifante who "knew much of the art of navigation . . . " Although the expedition did not reach the tip of Africa, it provided a lesson in wind and route. Correa wrote:

> Thus he always ran along the coast of Guiné, because he always navigated in sight of land, taking soundings, and writing down all he saw . . . He proceeded as far as that the coast began to turn seaward, and met with contrary winds, and struggled on, tacking frequently, now towards the land and now towards the sea, with such great storms and high seas, that they threatened to swallow up his ships. When he saw that the winds were general, without ever changing, and as four months had passed that they were beating about to landward and seaward, and that going out to sea he found the waves so great that he could not navigate amongst them wih the caravels . . .

A complaining crew and shortage of supplies forced the expedition to turn back to Portugal. But the voyage had revealed brutal facts. Janifante informed the king:

> If he were to take tall ships with which he could stand out more to sea, that he could go much farther on . . . that with large ships which could resist the waves, he could by beating up, run along the coast until he discovered the cape . . .

Gaspar Correa wrote that the king heeded the advice and commanded that the tall ships be built, but that Janifante died during the project.[8]

The next doubling of the end of Africa was the most celebrated one of all. The expedition was led by the iron willed Vasco da Gama. His fleet of four ships, S. Gabriel, S. Rafael, Berrio and a store ship rounded the cape and reached Calecut. There are extant several versions of the voyage. One was probably written by one of these three men: Alvaro Velho, Gonçalo Pires or João de Sá. It reports that the expedition left Portugal on July 8, 1497.

The first port of call was Santiago in the Cape Verde

Islands. Repairs were made and supplies were taken aboard. On August 3, the fleet was again under way, but some 200 leagues from Santiago the main yard of the S. Gabriel broke. All ships delayed while it was mended. On August 22, while on a course South by West, birds were sighted. Then some 800 leagues at sea, a whale was reported. On November 4, the fleet sighted land, and four days later anchored in a bay they named Santa Helena. They were on the west coast of Africa about 100 miles north of Cape Town.[9]

Another rendition of the voyage was written by the same Gaspar Correa. After reaching Cape Verde, reported Correa, they

> stood well out to sea to make the coast, which they knew they would find, as it advanced much seawards, as they learned from the sailors who had been in the caravels of Janifante; and they ran as far as they could to sea in the direction of the wind, to double the land without difficulty; and thus they navigated until they made the coast, and having reconnoitred it, they tacked and stood out to sea, hauling on the bowline as much as they could, and so they ran for many days. And as it seemed to them that now they could double the land, they again tacked towards the coast, also on the bowline, against the wind, until they again saw the coast.

The master then decided that their ships were farther south than Janifante's had ever been, and again they stood out to sea. There was little sun and the sea was angry but they continued on the same tack for a whole month. Again they put about and sailed for the land but this time the land was changed. It ran out to sea. All hands were confused and exhausted. The pilots announced that the land had no end, that it continued all the way across the sea. Vasco da Gama had no patience with speculation. He ordered the ships to put about and again to sail out to sea. They would remain on this tack, he added, until they could make the cape. When the crew begged for mercy, the commander "comported himself very angrily, swearing that if they did not double the cape, he would stand out to sea again as many times until the cape was doubled, or there should happen whatever should please God." When they tacked back toward land, they sailed into calmer seas, but there was no land. They had rounded the Cape of Good Hope. After a day's run they at last gazed upon mountains. Thence the da Gama fleet sailed on to India.[10]

It has been suggested that after this voyage Vasco da Gama drew up instructions on how to double the Cape of Good Hope. There is no doubt that the "Memorandum attributed to Vasco da Gama" contains such instructions but a great deal of doubt as to who wrote them. It is possible that Pedrálvares Cabral used these instructions while sailing for Calecut—which included a stop in Brazil.

The "Memorandum" recommends a stop in Santiago, Cape Verde Islands, where among other preparations a four month supply of water should be taken aboard. Then, with the wind well astern the course should be southerly, or if anything else, "let it be to the South-West." Upon reaching a light wind, the ship must put about and sail for the cape.[11]

In the telling of the Cabral voyage to India, familiar words appear. João de Barros wrote that Cabral stayed well off Guinea to avoid calms and "stood well out to sea to be certain of rounding the Cape of Good Hope." He continued "on that long tack" for a whole month, and on April 24, "they encountered another coast of land, which according to the pilots could have been 450 leagues west of the Guinea coast in the latitude of the

Antarctic Pole at 100 degrees."[12] The pilots were confused about their latitude, but this would not be the
last time Brazil would be placed somewhere in An-
tarctica.

In special letters to King Manuel I, the pilots described
the landfall and their bewilderment. Pedro Vaz de Caminha recorded that they had come upon "first a very
high rounded mountain, then other lower ranges of hills
to the south of it. . . (and) the Admiral named the mountain Easter Mount, and the country the Land of the True
Cross."[13]

Another pilot, Master John, wrote the king describing
the heavens, navigation and the disagreement among the
pilots as to where they were. At one point they differed
150 leagues, more than 450 nautical miles. Moreover,
Master John admitted that he was incapable of taking
an accurate reading at sea, even when the ship was
barely rolling.[14]

Master John was probably attempting to use an astrolabe. The astrolabe of 1500 was rather useless at sea for
it used an artificial horizon. The instrument had to be
held perpendicular to the horizon, not an easy feat while
standing or even while being held on a pitching rolling
deck.[15]

In his account of Vasco da Gama's first voyage, João
de Barros recounted that at Santa Helena Bay the Captain Major went ashore to "take the sun's altitude: because as there was but a short time since mariners of this
realm took advantage of the use of the astrolabe for that
requirement of navigation, and as the ships were small,
they did not put much trust in using them on account
of the ship's pitching and tossing."[16]

What was lacking in the astrolabe was not made up in
the charts. They offered little aid. In his letter to Don

Manuel, Master John quipped that the India charts between the Canaries and Cape Verde were so bad that
even Don Manuel would have laughed.
However confused all hands may have been, Pedrálvares Cabral's expedition had touched Brazil at 16° 20'
Lat. S. and 39° Long. W. about five miles north of
Porto Seguro or Baía Cabrália. Antonio Galvão in
Tratado dos Descobrimentos wrote that one ship was sent
off to examine the nearby bay. It was found to be "good
and safe" and thus was called Porto Seguro.[17]

N O T E S

1) João de Barros, *Primeira Década da Asia* (Lisboa: Livrarias
Aillaud e Bertrand, 1921), Déc. I, Liv. V, Caps. I e II, pp.
89-101.

> "A qual armada era de treze velas, entre naus, navios e car-
> velas cujos capitaes eram estes: Pedrálvares Cabral, capi-
> tãomor . . . Nicolau Coelho, que fôra com Vasco da Gama;
> Bartolomeu Dias, o que descobriou o Cabo do Boa Es-
> perança . . . " p. 93.

2) Barros, *Premeira Década*, Dec. I, Liv. III, cap. IV, p. 50.

> "Ao qual Bartolomeu Dias, e os de sua companhia, por
> causa dos perigos e tormentos que em o dobrar dêle pas-
> saram, ihe puserem nome Tormentoso; mas el-rei D. João,
> umdo êles ao Reino, ihe deu outro nome mais ilustre cha-
> mado-ihe Cabo de Boa Esperança, pela que êle prometia
> dêste descobrimento da India tão esperada, e por tantos
> anos requerida."

Diário da Viagem de Vasco da Gama, série Ultramarina, No. IV,
Livaria Civilização-Editora (Porto: Livraria Civilização), 1945,
p. 10.

3) *The Three Voyages of Vasco da Gama and His Viceroyalty from
the Lendas da India of Gaspar Correa accompanied by original
documents*, translation and notes by Hon. Henry E. J. Stanley.
The Hakluyt Society, ser. I, vol. 42. (New York: Burt Franklin),
pp. xxvii, 176, 228, 258.

4) *Portuguese Voyages 1498-1663*. Edited by Charles David Ley.

(London: J. M. Dent & Sons Ltd, 1947), "Letter of Pedro Vaz de Caminha written in Porto-Seguro of Vera Cruz on the First Day of May in the year 1500" pp. 41-59, p. 41.

5) J. H. Parry, *The Age of Reconnaissance,* (London: Weisenfeld and Nicolson, 1963), pp. 59-61.

6) Rear Admiral Boyle T. Somerville, *Ocean Passages for the World,* (London: Hydrographic Society Department, Admiralty, 1950), Sailing Ship Routes, pp. 225-229.

Byron's Journal of his Circumnavigation, 1764-1766, Edited by Robert Gallagher (Cambridge: University Press, for the Hakluyt Society, ser. II, vol, 122, 1964), n. p. 18.

Robert Gallagher states that many journals point out that the NE Trade wind is "deflected by the projection of Cape Verd to the westward, and that ships which keep near the coast of Africa lose the Trade sooner than others which are at a greater distance from the coast". For this reason many commanders recommend staying west when the NE Trade fails in order to continue it longer and have less calms and "baffling winds, in the variable space, and to meet the south-east Trade wind sooner than if farther east." By sailing this far west more than one ship has made the Brazil coast, thus "obliged to tack to the eastward, which occasioned considerable delay."

p. 25, Sir John Byron recorded in his Journal in Rio de Janeiro, "Whilst we lay here Lord Clive put in, in the Kent India Man who had sailed from England a Month before us & had touched no where..." Lord Clive was on his way to India.

7) *The Three Voyages of Vasco da Gama,* pp. 12-13.
Barros, *Premeira Década da Asia,* Dec. I, Liv. III Cap. IV, p. 49.

"E porque João Infante, capitão do navio S. PANTALEAO, foi o primeiro que saíu em terra, houve o rio nome que ora tem, do Infante, donde se toraram, por a gente repetir seus queixumes."

8) *The Three Voyages of Vasco da Gama,* pp. 12-15.

9) *Diário da Viagem de Vasco da Gama,* p. 2.

"E pairamos com o traquete e papa dous d. e hua noute, e e xxij (22) do dito mes hindo na volta do mar ao sull e a quarta do sudeste achamos muitas aves feitas como garçoees e quando veo a noute tiravam contra a susoeste mto rrigas como aves q hiam pera trra e neste mesmo d. vimos hua balea e jsto bem oytocentas legoas em mar."

10) *The Three Voyages of Vasco da Gama,* pp. 44-45.

n. Another historian, Castanheda, wrote that the expedition sighted land, then stood out to sea, then tacked back and reached Santa Helena Bay.

11) William B. Greenlee, *The Voyage of Pedro Alvares Cabral to Brazil and India from contemporary documents and narratives* (London: The Hakluyt Society, 1938), p. 167, "Memorandum Attributed to Vasco da Gama."

12) Barros, *Primeira Década da Asia,* p. 95.

"Junta a frota que passou o temporal por fugir da terra de Guiné (onde as calmarias lhe podiam impedir seu caminho) empègou-se muito no mar, por lhe i ficar seguro poder dobrar O Cabo de Boa Esperança. E, havendo ja um mês que ia naquela grande volta, quando veio à segunda oitava da Páscoa (que eram 24 de Abril) foi dar em outra costa de terra firme, a qual, segundo a estimação dos pilotos lhe parecau que podia distar para aloeste da costa de Guiné 450 léguas, e em altura do polo Antártico da parte do Sul 10 graus."

13) Ley, *Portuguese Voyages,* p. 42.

14) Greenlee, *The Voyage of Pedro Alvares Cabral,* p. 36. "Letter of Master John to King Manuel" dated May 1, 1500, Vera Cruz.

15) Parry, *The Age of Reconnaissance,* p. 92.

16) *The Three Voyages of Vasco da Gama,* pp. 44-45.

n. quote from Barros' Asia, dec. I. liv. IV, cap. II.

17) Antonio Galvão, *Tratado dos Descobrimentos Antiguos e Modernos,* (Porto: Livraria Civilização—1963), p. 148.

"E mandou o capitam môr hum nauio apalpar se achaua porto tornou, dizendo, que achaua bom e seguro, e assi lhe poserão o nome."

CHAPTER III

BRAZIL

Was Cabral aware of the place we call Brazil before
he reached it? Some argue that he had been instructed to
sail farther into the west than his predecessors and seek or
claim the land lying there. To date, no one has been able
to document this story. Just as some have been unable to
prove that the 16th century discovery of Brazil was definitely an accident, others have not shown that it was the
result of careful planning, or a rediscovery.

No one can flatly deny that the great continent in the
West could have been sighted on an earlier day. Stories
about it survive to this day. One, first told in 1535 by
Oviedo, recounted that Christopher Columbus, while
living in Lisbon, sheltered a Spanish pilot named Sanchez
who told of land in the West. Sanchez had sailed West
from Madeira, sighted land, then been shipwrecked. It
was said that he told Columbus about this place before
he expired in his house in 1484.[1]

There is an unending procession of tales about imagi-
nary islands in the Atlantic: St. Brenden's Isles, Mayda,
Satanaxes, Brazil and Antillia, to name but a few. In
1462 Afonso II declared that he would give two of the
St. Brenden's Isles to a Sr. Vogado if he could find them.[2]
Contact through commerce and the printed word had

elaborated and spread the stories about the islands in the West. For many years via the Atlantic coastal trade, the Straits of Gibraltar, and the parade of merchants travelling overland to the trade fairs of Europe, Portugal had been in touch with Northern Europe, the Mediterranean and the Levant.[3] Under the guiding hand of the Infante Henry her influence in Africa had expanded to the South. Many of the tales about mysterious islands were simply and informally told by captains and merchants. Many of these words were never recorded.

For years maps had shown but little of the unknown "Sea of Darkness" with numerous imagined islands scattered about. Brazil was among them. In his *Admiral of the Ocean Sea,* S. E. Morison wrote that in about 1480 Bristol mariners began "to search for the mythical island of O'Brasil off Ireland, which people have sworn that they saw even in the last century."[4] In Ireland *Hy Brazil* is a fanciful heaven on earth, or a dream land or island. O'Brazil or O'Brassell is an Irish surname found in County Liumneach. Through the years fact and fable merged. In a speech to the American Antiquarian Society in 1873, E. E. Hale informed his audience that the Island of Bresil was still on the Admiralty Charts, right on the New York-London steamer route![5]

In *The Vinland Map and the Tartar Relation,* R. A. Skelton recorded that in the Middle Ages there were probably two northern sailing routes: the Norsemen route from Norway to Iceland to Greenland or directly from Norway to Greenland, and a southern Summer and Fall route which took advantage of the seasonal northeasterly winds. Perhaps it was on this route that Bristol merchants sought the island of Brazil or "Brasylle" somewhere west of Ireland. Some maintain that in years before 1494 the English found the Brazil we know while searching for their imaginary island.[6] There seems to be no substantial proof for this argument, but there is no reason to consider the voyage impossible.

Continental Brazil, although earlier still sometimes called an island, appeared on Juan de la Cosa's *Mapamundi*, dated 1500. It was entitled *"Isla descubierta por Portugal que puede aludir al Brasil por su tamaño y latitud aunque está muy al Este."*[7] Juan de la Cosa was probably describing the land Cabral had found, and about which he had immediately informed the king. It has also been suggested that Juan de la Cosa revised this map but did not give the dates of revision. On the same *Mapamundi,* Cuba is shown as an island. It was not circumnavigated until 1508.[8]

Brazil in South America, complete with red parrots, and trees, appears on the 1502 Cantino Planisphere. Cabo de Sam Jorge and Porto Seguro are named, and there is a short description of the discovery of Porto Seguro. Except for the land near Cabral's landfall, the coast is drawn in outline. Later a bay and more names were added to the map, but the 1502 version was probably based on the letters which Gaspar de Lemos took back from Porto Seguro and the 1501 João de Nova expedition to India. There are documents stating that he stopped in Brazil en route to India and then named Cabo de Sam Jorge. Also shown on the Cantino map is the Line of Demarcation 370 leagues West of the Cape Verde Islands, Brazil, lying East of that line, was legally Portuguese. John II and his diplomats had been more clever than even they had imagined.[9]

NOTES

1) Justin Winsor, *Narrative and Critical History of America by a corps of eminent historical scholars and specialists under the editorship of Justin Winsor.* vol. II, *Spanish Exploration and Settlements on America from the Fifteenth century to the Seventeenth century,* (Boston: Houghton Mifflin and Co., 1886), p. 33. see Gago Coutinho, *O Descobrimento do Brasil* (Lisbon: Sociedade de Geografia, 197), pp. 16.

2) Samuel Eliot Morison, *Admiral of the Ocean Sea, A Life of Christopher Columbus* (Boston: Little, Brown and Co. 1942) p. 58.

   R. A. Skelton, *Explorers' Maps, Chapters in the Cartograhic Record of Geographical Discovery,* (London: Routledge and Kegan Paul, 1958), p. 52.

   In various forms Brazil and other real and imaginary islands had appeared and disappeared on maps and charts. Indeed, the Atlantic Ocean was punctuated with islands, rocks and reefs. In a 1455 Portolano chart by Bartolomeu Pareto, one gets a taste of the many islands such as: Insulle de Inforno, Insulle Fortunate, Sãct Brandanv and Insulle de Brazíl.

   On the Pareto chart the other two islands are: Insulle de Inferno and Insulle de Brazil.

3) Bailey W. Diffie, *Prelude to Empire: Portugal Overseas before Henry the Navigator,* (Lincoln: University of Nebraska Press, 1960), pp. 1-48.

4) Morison, *Admiral of the Ocean Sea,* p. 58.

5) Winsor, *Narrative and Critical History,* p. 36.

6) R. A. Skelton, Thomas E. Marston, George D. Painter, *The Vinland Map and Tartar Relation,* (New Haven: Yale University Press, 1965), p. 234.

   On the Vinland Map one sees *Magnae Insulae Beati Brandani Branziliae dictae. Insulae Sancti Brandini* had often applied to the Azores and Madeira. The Vinland Map was the first map to move it to the west and apply it to the Antilla group. The name Branziliae, which reminds one of the imaginary Bresil, is not in any other surviving map. The names Brazil, Brasil, Bersil, Brazir, Bracir and Brazilli in the 14th and 15th centuries referred to an island off Ireland, which is not mentioned in medieval Irish literature. p. 138, Map VII.

Islands named Brasil and Mayda or Man (bersil and ventura in Bianco's atlas) had become standardized in cartography before the end of the 14th century, p. 157.

Edward MacLysaght, *Irish Families, their Names, Arms and Origins* (Dublin: Hodges, Figgis and Co., Ltd., 1957) p. 310. GAELIC IRISH SURNAMES WHICH HAVE A FOREIGN APPEARANCE BUT ARE NEVERTHELESS RARELY IF EVER FOUND INDIGENOUS OUTSIDE IRELAND include the name — *Brazil*.

A letter from the Bishop of the Diocese of Liumneach's secretary reports that HY BRAZIL can be described as "a sort of fanciful heaven on earth, existing in the minds of poets, a dream land or island."

As for the surname BRASSILL, the Bishop's secretary wrote that it is a surname found in County Liumneach. Some of the English renderings of this Gaelic name are: O' Brassell, O' Brazil, Brassill, Brazil, Brazel. It apparently is a "rare and scattered surname." It has been suggested that the original name meant: "descendant of BREASAL, meaning strife or war."

In the Dublin telephone directory there are the names Brassil and Brassill, and 15 spelled Brazil.

7) Mapamundi, *Juan de la Cosa*, seen in the Atlas *MAPAS ESPANOLES DE AMERICA* published by the Spanish government in 1951. The original map is in the Museo Naval, Madrid.

8) Skelton, *Explorers' Maps*, p. 71.

9) Skelton, *Explorers' Maps*, pp. 31, 72. The western portion of the Cantino World Map is on p. 58.

Copy of a Letter of the King of Portugal Sent to the King of Castile Concerning the Voyage and Success of India, trans. by Sergio J. Pacifici, (Minneapolis: The University of Minnesota Press, 1955). The first printed reference to the discovery of Brazil was distributed in Rome, October 28, 1505.

Whether it was truly a letter from the Portuguese monarch or simply a news item has not been definitely decided. It was of great importance, regardless. On the Cabral expedition:

"The first ships we sent to those lands were twelve in number, plus a caravel full of provisions. These ships left Lisbon in the year 1500, on the 8th day of March to go and trade in spices and drugs in the land of India beyond the Red and Persian Seas, to a city called Calicut ... Pedro Alvares Cabral was the Captain General of the afore-mentioned armada. Sailing past Cape Verde, they sighted a land which had recently come to be known in our Europe, to which they gave the name of Santa Cruz, and this because they had a very high cross erected on its shore. Others call it New Land, that is, New World. This land where they came ashore is situated on the 14th meridian beyond the Tropic of Cancer, as the sailors found its position by means of their quadrants and astrolabes, since they sail in those parts with astrological instruments. The land is situated 400 leagues west of the afore-mentioned Cape Verde." pp. 3-4.

Donald Weinstein, *Ambassador from Venice, Pietro Pasqualigo in Lisbon, 1501,* (Minneapolis: The University of Minnesota Press, 1960), pp. 58-59. "Two important accounts (of the discovery of Brazil) were those of the Venetian representatives in Lisbon.

Il Cretico, the Venetian nuncio, called it UNA TERRA NUOVA and said that it was believed to be mainland because the expedition sailed along the coast for more than a thousand miles without finding the end, a contention which seems to have been erroneous. Pisani, the ambassador, also called it TERRA NUOVA and mainland. What this new found continent or island was believed to be none of the informants tells us, and it seems safe to assume that they had no idea of its true nature."

Armando Cortesão and Avelino Teixeira da Mota, *Portugaliae Monumenta Cartographica,* (Lisboa, 1960), Vol. 1, pp. 10-11.

CHAPTER IV

L' ESPOIR

Not far behind Pedrálvares Cabral was a Norman, Binot Paulmier de Gonneville.[1] His voyage was a confused one and has baffled historians ever since. His destination was India. The inspiration for the journey was sparked in Lisbon where Binot and two companions, Jean l'Anglois and Pierre le Carpentier, had looked in wonder at a spectacular sight, a mariner's dream. There, anchored in the mouth of the Tejo River, were Portuguese caravelas laden with spices and rare things. They were the ships of the Vasco da Gama expedition, just returned from the grueling voyage to Calecut.

The three Normans soon decided to send their own ship to trade in the Orient. Before leaving Lisbon, they hired two Portuguese pilots, Bastian Moura and Diogo Cohinto, for high wages. These pilots were in a position to demand excellent wages, for they had sailed to India, something which in 1502 few had done. In accepting positions on a Norman vessel the Portuguese were gambling with more than the elements. The King of Portugal discouraged the giving away or selling of Portuguese routes or charts to foreigners. An Italian agent in Lisbon reported that charts were scarce as the penalty for removing them from Portugal was death.[2]

Binot Paulmier de Gonneville's expedition is remind-
ing of Cabral's: while sailing for the Cape of Good Hope,
Gonneville encountered Brazil. He considered this an
unfortunate accident. Disappointed as he was, this, nevertheless, was the earliest recorded contact between France
and America. It perplexed French navigators, geographers and historians for nearly three and one half centuries. In fact, it was not until recent years that there was
agreement that Gonneville was even in Brazil. This came
with the discovery of an excerpt from a long lost official
declaration of the voyage. According to law, upon returning from his voyage Gonneville and his officers had
presented a declaration to the Admiralty Court in Rouen.

Binot Paulmier belonged to a noble family of Buschet
in the parish of Gonneville-les-Honfleur in the bailiwick
of Rouen and diocese of Lisieux. Soon after Gonneville
and his companions determined to make the voyage to
India, they realized that they did not have sufficient
funds to finance so ambitious an enterprise. They enlisted
capital from six others: Etienne and Antoine Thiéry,
Andrieu de la Mere, Batiste Bourgeoz, Thomas Athinal
and Jean Carrey. All were bourgeois; all were from
Honfleur.[3]

The nine entrepreneurs then purchased and equipped
the ship *l'Espoir,* probably a carrack type design. She
was a vessel of 120 ton capacity, and had voyaged only
once before—to Hamburg. She was described as being of
sound hull, carrying good sails, with some of the best
rigging in the Honflleur harbor. Her owners reported
that they provisioned her well.

L'Espoir was armed with two cannons and two demi-
pieces of ordinary copper and latten; six smaller pieces
and mortars made of iron, and 40 muskets, harquebuses
and other light arms.[4] For ammunition the owners had

put aboard 1600 pounds of different calibre balls, 3 dozen of them with bars and chains attached for blasting holes in the hulls of enemy ships. Another 900 pounds of ammunition consisted of more balls and scraps and bits of iron. Down in the hold were 2000 bags of cannon powder (one fifth of it granulated), wicks, match, rammers, sights and carriages for mounting the cannon. Cannon cartridge was of iron, parchment skin and thick paper. Hand to hand combat weapons were pikes, halberds and daggers.

L'Espoir carried naval stores of extra anchors, cables, tiller and bar. She was loaded with a two year supply of food: ship's biscuit, grain, flour, peas, lard, salted and dried goat meat and fish. Ciders, other drinks (unnamed) and a year's supply of water made up her supply of liquids.[5] How long the water would be potable was anyone's guess. Most northern Europeans carried their water in casks, and it did not take long for it to be rendered foul. Far more effective was the Arab practice of using open tanks on deck which were constantly refreshed by air and rain water.[6]

Also put aboard *l'Espoir* were sundry articles for trade with the merchants and monarchs of the Orient. The list is not impressive. Did the Portuguese pilots not speak of the wealth and sophistication of Calecut to the Norman entrepreneurs? Perhaps the Normans did not believe their stories. Or perhaps the investors could not afford to purchase such costly goods for trade. Possibly they thought they could outbargain the Indian merchants.

One reads in wonder but not implicit belief Gaspar Correa's description of the articles the da Gama expedition carried for trade with the Sheikhs at Mozambique, Ouilea, Melinde, and finally Calecut. The wealth the

Moors displayed was no less impressive. Correa reported that they were seated on elaborate gold and ivory stools.

Apparently their wealth was so overwhelming that the Portuguese felt compelled to boast or at least indicate that they too were rich and powerful and were something to be reckoned with. Correa wrote that at Melinde, Nicolas Coelho told the Sheikh that the King of Portugal had "many thousand horsemen . . . a fleet of 200 ships . . . so many cities and towns, and . . . such revenues, that every month he put into his treasury two hundred thousand cruzados beyond his expenditure . . . " To support such descriptions, Vasco da Gama sent the Sheikh at Melinde "a piece of scarlet cloth . . . and a large mirror of Flanders closed with doors, and beautifully gilt."

Luis Vaz de Camões, c. 1524-1580, the poet chronicler of Portugal's glory, in his epic poem, *The Lusiads,* painted a breathtaking scene of Vasco da Gama meeting the Sheikh of Melinde.

> *Nor less of pomp the Lusitanian*
> *   shows*
> *When, with his gallant retinue,*
> *   advance*
> *The armada's boats, midway to*
> *   welcome those*
> *Of the Melindian on the bay's*
> *   expanse.*
> *Clad in the vogue of Spain*
> *   Da Gama goes,*
> *All but the cloak, a gorgeous*
> *   robe of France,*
> *The web Venetian satin, and the*
> *   dye*
> *A glorious crimson that delights*
> *   the eye.*[7]

Canto II, 97, Quillinan, trans.

In Calecut even the simple fishermen were aware of the difference between valuable and worthless reward. Correa wrote that when they were paid for fish with vintins, "they bit with their teeth to see if it was silver."[8]

But not all historians agreed with Gaspar Correa. João de Barros wrote that Vasco da Gama took no presents along because he was not certain that he would ever reach India. That does not sound like the captain major who "comported himself very angrily" when his crew began to be fearful of the voyage around the cape. Fernão de Castenheda also recorded that da Gama voyaged without presents for the eastern monarchs, and that when the Moor asked for his statue of the Virgin Mary, he refused claiming that he needed it for protection at sea, and that it was only gilded wood anyway.[9]

The little ship *l'Espoir* carried few things better than gilded wood for trade in the Orient.

 300 pieces of various material:
        some hatchets, spades, bill hooks, plows, double-edge
        slashers for mowing (machetes), all together 4000
2000 pine cones
  50 dozen little mirrors
   6 quintas (100 kilos) of imitation pearls
   8 quintas of old hardware from Rouen
  20 gross of knives and pocket knives
        a bale of pins and needles
  20 pieces of woolen material
  30 pieces of fustian, a coarse cloth of cotton and linen
   4 pieces of scarlet cloth
   8 other pieces of different styles
        one of velours with design
        some others of gilded cloth
        inconsequential money which they knew was more ac-
           ceptable in India than gold
        and finally, all the same, things the Portuguese were accus-
           tomed to carrying for the best trading over there and en
           route[10]

Unfortunately the declaration of the voyage of the *l'Espoir* did not elaborate on the goods the Portuguese were accustomed to carrying. A later account on the tragic sinking of the Portuguese ship *Santiago* in 1585 mentioned cloth, tin and beads on board for trade in Africa.[11]

Sixty men voyaged on *l'Espoir*. According to the declaration, "all (were) of goodwill especially the bourgeois of the ship, the captain-commander, the said Gonneville, to command the voyage as best he could with the advice of Andrieu de la Mare and Antoine Thiéry."

On Saint John the Baptist's Day, June 24, 1503, the Normans sailed out of Honfleur harbor. All hands had received the sacraments of the church for they did not know if they would ever see Normandy again. Some would not.

There is little doubt that the pilots chose to sail out to sea as da Gama and Cabral had done. The first entry in the declaration described wind "that just skimmed over the sea . . . northeast and favorable." An 18 day voyage took them to the Canary Islands where they did not put in but sailed between the lofty Tenerife and Gomera Islands, then on to Barbary which they described as low and dry.[12]

From Barbary they sailed on to the mountainous Cape Verde Islands, populated by goat raising Portuguese. The next call, a 10 day stop, was at Cap Verde where they replenished supplies, took on fresh water, and for the first time tasted Moorish cous-cous.

On August 9, *l'Espoir* sailed away from Cap Verde and out to sea to escape "the dangers and pestilence" of the African coast. For six weeks the wind was generally favorable, broken by great whirlwinds in otherwise perfectly calm waters, but these were brief. The officers reported that these strange tornados were accompanied by frequent "uncomfortable stinking rain which soiled clothing, tore at the skin and caused infection."[13]

Possibly the crew of *l'Espoir* were victims of the conflict between the harmattan and the monsoon, still to be observed in whirlwinds which spring up out of a calm sea as many as 200 miles off the coast of Africa. The London Hydrographic Department's *Africa Pilot* describes these tornados as "heralded by the amassing of cumulonimbus cloud, coppery and livid by day, excessively black by night, out of which lightning emanates . . ." This cloud moves on a broad front, a squall with violent whipping wind, lightning and thunder. High above the earth where the harmattan never ceases to blow, great clouds of red African soil have been observed.[14] The "stinking" uncomfortable rain no doubt contained soil as well as reeds, fish and whatever else the swirling wind had swept up from the sea. A later voyager, Sir John Byron, while off the west coast of Africa logged, ". . . we are under hourly apprehensions of a tornado which might prove of fatal consequence to ships in this bay (Porto da Praia, Cape Verde Islands), as they are extremely violent . . . No ships ever come in here after the 15th of August til the rainy season is over which is generally in November . . ."[15]

With the whirlwinds behind them, the Normans sailed over the equator on September 12, 1503. They saw and caught flying fish, porpoise and various other fish. Now the sailors were struck with scurvy. Two thirds of the crew suffered from it, and several men died.

The little ship now looked to the Southern Cross as her guide. For the month of October she was alone, apparently sailing without event. About November 9th the crew sighted seaweed, "long and thick reeds with their

roots which the Portuguese said was a sign of the Cape
of Good Hope." These, the French scholar, André Julien,
ventures were perhaps rush or cane which grows in African rivers and could float out to sea.[16] Cold days and
"Manche de Velours," penguins common in the South
Atlantic, led the pilots to believe that the ship was well
south of the cape, but they never had the opportunity to
verify this. On about November 30 *l'Espoir* was deluged
by "contrary" winds, and for three weeks she could hardly make way. To make matters worse, one of the pilots,
Collin Vasseur, died. *L'Espoir* had lost her way, was in
need of water, "at the mercy of the sea."

Then the contrary wind, indeed all the wind, ceased
to blow, and *l'Espoir* drifted in a calm. More birds,
seen in the south, cheered all hands. This surely was a
sign of land. The pilots decided to steer for it. The brief
declaration does not reveal the ship's course or position,
but merely reports: "in order to turn away from East
India, the ship had to be brought about." When the
course was changed or how long the new course was sailed
remains a mystery, but on January 5, 1504, Captain
Gonneville's expedition came upon "une grande terre."
The following day the Normans went ashore. A small
boat sent for reconnaissance brought news of a nearby
river. *L'Espoir* sailed into it, and the homesick Normans
thought of their own River Orne.

But there was no time for longing for home. The bat-
tered ship was in need of repair, and the tattered crew
were restless and discontented. They announced that they
must return to France and would certainly not sail on to
India. For one thing, the chief pilot had been lost, and
for another, they doubted that *l'Espoir* would even
float as far as India. Gonneville was forced to acquiesce.

It did not take long for curious Indians to appear or

for the Normans to develop an interest in their hunting, fishing, houses, government and customs. These Indians, perhaps Guaranis, were ruled by a chief, Arosca, a widower of some 60 years, father of six sons. Arosca, in the throes of war with his neighbors, soon perceived that these white strangers could afford him considerable advantage over his enemies. During their stay, the Normans twice transported some 600 Indians to war in *l'Espoir*. All the Indians, friend or foe, were in awe of the Normans' cannon and ship. The inevitable trading soon began: mirrors, combs, knives, and Rouen hardware in exchange for meat, fish, skins, and magnificent plumes. Their cargo was in demand and they anticipated a fine profit for the skins and plumes in France.

On Easter Sunday, April 7, Europeans and Indians joined together in a ceremony commemorating *l'Espoir's* visit to that strange land. A wooden cross 35 feet high, bearing the names of the pope, the Admiral of France, and the captain of *l'Espoir* was erected.

With the ship repaired, and the anxious crew again in good health, all made ready for the homeward voyage. There were two new voyagers on board: Essomericq, one of Arosca's sons, and Namoa, a companion and tutor. For the Normans' own chief, Louis XII, Arosca sent gifts of plumes and other rare things.

The declaration does not reveal whether the French suggested that Essomericq return to France with them to taste their civilization or if Arosca requested that he take the voyage. It reports that Arosca was overjoyed that the French wished to have the Indians aboard. Essomericq would enter Christendom, and, by the way, learn about artillery, thus enabling his tribe to "master their enemies." The Normans would return with special souvenirs and exhibits, and Essomericq would study abroad. He would rejoin his father, the French promised, in twenty moons.

On July 3, 1504, *l'Espoir's* sails were raised and she was turned toward the sea. On shore the Indians gave a hearty farewell cheer, and making the sign of the cross with their fingers, again promised the mariners that they would preserve the wooden cross planted on their shores.[17]

Whatever the course, the return voyage was no more comfortable than the voyage out had been. Fever struck again and took the ship's surgeon, a soldier from Honfleur, the captain's valet, and Namoa. Before the unlucky Indian succumbed, it was suggested that he be baptized, but Nicole Le Febvre, the most learned fellow on board, claimed it would not be proper as Namoa was totally ignorant of the dogma of Holy Church. Later, Essomericq too suffered from fever, but he was baptized Binot after the captain and given three godfathers: the captain, Antoine Thiéry and Andrieu de la Mare. The story is gloomy. Many were weak with fever; all were in desperate need of fresh water; the ship was foul.

Somehow, this pathetic ship carrying exhausted men sailed on and crossed the Tropic of Capricorn. Now, they concluded, *l'Espoir* was farther than ever from Africa, even farther than "the countries of the West Indies" where Normans and Bretons had sailed for dyewood, cotton, parrots, and monkeys. As the captain himself did not know his position, it is difficult to guess where earlier mariners had supposedly been trading; northern Brazil is a possibility.

Great gaps in time and place allow for speculation but little conclusion. About October 10th land was sighted, and *l'Espoir* steered for it, or, in search of fresh water and provisions, the ship was turned west and/or south, and then land was found. The Normans went ashore for provisions and found another tribe of Indians. These were simple people who painted their naked bodies, adorned their lips with polished green stones, fished, hunted, and unfortunately for the visitors, practiced cannibalism. While tramping about for supplies, several Normans lost their lives, among them the learned Nicole Le Febvre, a man "full of curiosity." The Normans departed at once and sailed 100 leagues north in search of a more agreeable place to reprovision the depleted ship. Again they landed, probably near Bahia, and now greeted by friendly Indians, they took on supplies and enough merchandise (or so they later claimed) to not only pay for the voyage, but to render a profit as well. They put two Indians on board, and for the third time departed Brazil. About nine miles at sea the Indians jumped overboard. Eight days later l'Espoir passed a wooded island perhaps Fernando de Noronha, and the ship was deluged with richly plumed birds. A southwester then blew and an encouraged crew found a welcomed guide, the North Star.

But the voyage was not yet over and the little ship pounded through more angry waters before reaching the latitude of the Canary Islands. At Fayol in the Portuguese Azores, she took on more supplies and fresh water, then set out on her final leg. But a storm forced her to put in again, this time in Ireland where the ship was repaired. Again the Normans started for home, but after a parade of misfortune, there was more. Near the islands of Jersey and Gurnsey, out sprang an English pirate, Edouard Blunth of Plymouth. At first there seemed hope of keeping the scoundrel off, but then appeared another sea wolf, this one a Breton, Mouris Fortin. Now with two fresh ships against one shabby hulk manned by a decimated crew, it was hardly a battle. Gonneville attempted a desperate escape, and raced for the coast in hopes of beaching the ship, but he, the crew and the ship were too weary, too slow. The pirates pillaged *l'Espoir*. Then they sank her.

Almost in sight of home, more Normans had lost their lives. Some of the wounded were left at The Hague. Only 28 returned to Honfleur. Gonneville, the brothers Thiéry, Andrieu de la Mare, and Essomericq-Binot were among the survivors, and no doubt thankful, but the cargo, the ship's log, indeed, the ship had been lost. Reparations were requested not only for those who had suffered through the voyage, but also for those who had risked their money. According to the law that the journals or declarations of all long voyages be delivered to the courts of justice, the officers of *l'Espoir* presented a declaration to the Admiralty Court in Rouen.[18]

Essomericq never again saw Brazil but remained with Gonneville and was brought up as a Frenchman and Christian. It was not revealed whether he approved of the behavior of the Normans once hailed by his people as "angels from heaven," but the adjustment apparently was not insurmountable as in 1521 he married Gonneville's daughter. When Captain Gonneville died, part of his estate was bequeathed to his son-in-law on the condition that his male descendents bore the name and arms of Gonneville.[19]

There the story of Gonneville might have ended. The family Gonneville might have again carried on an ordinary provincial life in the bailiwick of Rouen, had it not been for Essomericq's grandson, the Abbé Paulmier Gonneville. He decided that he had special capacity for missionary work, and that there was a reason for it. In a letter written in 1658 to Pope Alexander VII the abbé requested funds to teach the Gospel in the southern regions of the world and supported the request with the belief that Providence had allowed his grandfather to remain in France and become a Christian so that his grandson might return to his native land and enlighten his people.

The letter to Rome included the itinerary of the 1503-1505 voyage of *l'Espoir,* but in copying it from the original declaration, the abbé, for some reason, changed the wording. The difference was slight but sufficient to throw geographers and historians into confusion for nearly 200 years. According to the account the abbé sent Alexander VII:

> . . . the ship was outfitted at Honfleur near the mouth of the Seine. Mr. Gonneville, who was the commander of it weighed anchor in the month of June, 1503, and rounded the Cape of Good Hope, where he was assailed by a raging wind which caused him to lose his way and abandoned him in a dull calm.[20]

The bewilderment began with the very first interpretations of the abbé's request to proselytize in the southern regions of the world, "du monde austral." That, concluded some, was certainly Australia. In 1735, the Indies Company in search of a southern port of call, called upon competent navigators. Bouvet de Lozier announced that he would find one in Gonneville's land, but where was it? Geographers divined that it lay at about Lat. 42° South. Not willing to base a voyage of such magnitude upon rumor, Bouvet de Lozier requested the original declaration of the voyage of *l'Espoir* from Rouen, but was informed that no documents of this sort dated before 1600 were available. He decided to sail anyhow. All he found was "Terre de la Circoncision" and ice, a region which bore no resemblance to the lush land described by Captain Gonneville.[21]

Those who all along had insisted that Lat. 42° South was not where Gonneville's land was located rejoiced. One gentleman, a former governor of a town in Brittany, M. Benard de la Harpe, suspected that Gonneville had voyaged to Virginia. He had been there himself and remarked that the natives were similar to the Indians Gonneville had described.[22]

Throughout the 18th century, the speculation continued. Guesses ranged from the Moluccas, again to Australia, to the frozen waters of the south. In the late 18th century another navigator sought Gonneville's land as compensation for what France had lost in Canada. Captain Kerguelen found ice, and then for reasons he never revealed, suggested that Madagascar was Gonneville's land.[23]

Based upon the Abbé Gonneville's version of the voyage, the doubling of the cape, the "raging wind," Madagascar was not an unreasonable guess for the location of Gonneville's land. Only the original declaration would clear away the confusion. At last, in 1847, Pierre Margry, a French historian, uncovered part of a copy of the document which had escaped so many searchers. It was buried in the archives of the Ministry of the Navy, but again, because another Gonneville had tampered with a document, the facts were not accurate. This time the Baron de Gonneville had rewritten history.

After the explorer Kerguelen had returned from his fruitless voyage, some had begun to question the reliability of the Gonneville family. His honor at stake, a descendent of Abbé Gonneville, Baron de Gonneville, joined the search for the original declaration. The family house had been sold, but the baron gained entry, found the 1505 declaration, and soon perceived the abbé's version did not match the captain's. Baron de Gonneville then drew up a copy of the original declaration and sent it to the Ministry of the Navy. An employee of the archives accepted the document and reported that it matched the abbé's work. Mysteriously, the baron did not object. Later, the historian Pierre Margry uncovered the baron's copy, studied it and the abbé's account, and realized that they certainly were not the same. The baron's copy described not the rounding of the Cape of Good Hope, but rather that of Cape Saint Augustine, then sailing 600 leagues to the latitude of the Cape of Good Hope. Later, l'Espoir was rent by raging winds, and left drifting in a calm.[24]

The difference between in fact rounding and merely sailing at the latitude of the Cape of Good Hope was great enough to place Gonneville's land on another part of the globe. After reconstructing the voyage, Historian Margry concluded that l'Espoir had sailed to Brazil. His conclusions, not the last to be drawn, were published in 1867.

In January 1869 M. d'Avezac, an historian who had once published an article on Captain Gonneville, received a letter from the Keeper of the Bibliotheque d'Arsenal. More on l'Espoir had been unearthed. This time it was a second copy of the baron's account, and far more important, a textual extract of Captain Gonneville's original 1503 declaration. Here at last was the document upon which the abbé and the baron had based their versions of the story.

The textual extract was divided into two parts. The first contained information on the ship's equipment and the voyage. The second was the "Lettres Royaux" dated August 30, 1658. For some reason, probably taxation, the Gonnevilles feared that they were legally categorized as immigrants in France, and in the "Lettres Royaux" argued that their ancestor Essomericq was certainly not an immigrant. He had been promised a round trip. For proof the reader was referred to the story of Essomericq's departure from his native land. According to custom the original declaration had been claimed by the Gonneville family, then apparently lost. Only the textual extract remained.[25]

Through exhaustive research on the extract, Pierre Margry, Armand d'Avezac, and more recently, André Julien, reached the same general conclusions about the voyage of *l'Espoir*. During the voyage there was great hardship and confusion. There were tornados, calms, discouragement, suffering. It is hardly surprising that the ship wandered about completely lost on the voyage out from France. It is not unlikely that she was farther from the Cape of Good Hope than her pilots ever dreamed. Perhaps the reeds and birds were from the Island of Tristan d'Acunha. If *l'Espoir* had sailed west from that position, it would have been difficult for her to have avoided Brazil.[26]

As for the time factor, we too are left confused. On November 9th the Portuguese took floating weeds to be signs of the Cape of Good Hope. About November 30, there were words that contrary winds had nearly halted progress for three weeks. Then with no mention of dates the little ship tossed in the sea, birds were sighted to the south (another sign of land?), and the stern was turned to the East Indies. On January 5, land was found. Between November 9, and January 5, there were two reports of signs of land and one landfall. *L'Espoir* with a crew weakened and baffled could have been sailing in the Horse Latitudes, crossing and re-crossing contrary winds, currents, calms. At any given time we are igorant as to what course she was following.

Perhaps the first signs of land floated from Africa, or from Tristan d'Acunha. The second signs might have been from Tristan d'Acunha, Trindade, Martin Vaz, or even Brazil.

We know that *l'Espoir* turned away from the east, but not when. That the Normans landed at Brazil at about 26° 10° South Latitude near the mouth of the Rio São Francisco is perfectly possible.[27] Thus *l'Espoir,* like some before her and many after, had struck Brazil while attempting to tack for the Cape of Good Hope.

NOTES

1) André Julien, *Les Français en Amérique pendant la première moîtié du XVI siècle, Textes des Voyages de Gonneville, Verrazano, J. Cartier et Roberval.* intro. par Ch. A. Julien (Paris: Presses Universitaires de France, 1946), pp. 25-45.

As the textual extract referred to was removed from the archives during World War II and as of M. Julien's writing, had not yet reappeared, M. Julien used the reproduction in M. d'Avezac's book.

Campagne du Navire l'Espoir de Honfleur 1503-5, Relation Authentique du Voyage du Capitaine de Gonneville ès nouvelles Terres des Indes, publiée intégralement pour la premiere fois avec une introduction et des éclaircissements par M. d'Avezac, (Paris: Challamel, 1869), pp. 87-115.

For this source both d'Avezac and Julien were consulted. M. P. Lacroix found the document in the Arsenal. In d'Avezac's book, and thus in Julien's are copies of manuscript 3221 (24 ter H.F.) of the Bibliothèque de l'Arsenal, papier 12 feuillets, 210 x 150 millimètres écriture du XVII siècle.

The letter which Abbé Gonneville sent the Pope was first published in *Mémoires touchant l'establissement d'une Mission Chrétienne dans la Terre Australe* (Paris: 1863) printed by Cramoisy 1663, signed J.P.D.C. Prête Indien.

2) R. A. Skelton, *Explorers' Maps*, pp. 31-33.
3) d'Avezac, *Campagne du Navire l'Espoir*, p. 7.
   Julien, *Français en Amérique*, extract, p. 26.
4) Julien, *Français en Amérique*, extract, pp. 26, 27.
   The canons were probably muzzle loading cast canon which could send a ball about 300 yards.
5) Julien, *Français en Amérique*, extract, pp. 28-29.
6) *The Three Voyages of Vasco da Gama*, p. 139, quote from Gaspar Correa.
7) *The Three Voyages of Vasco da Gama*, pp. 119-122, from Gaspar Correa, and p. 122, "Os Lusiadas," Canto II, translated by Quillinan.
8) *The Three Voyages of Vasco da Gama*, p. 150.
9) *The Three Voyages of Vasco da Gama*, pp. 173-174.
10) Julien, *Français en Amérique*, extract, pp. 29-30.
11) Ley, *Portuguese Voyages,* from the *Tragic History of the Sea,* "Account of the wreck of the Santiago in the year 1585" by Manoel Godino Cardoso, p. 283.
12) Julien, *Les Français en Amérique*, extract, p. 30.
13) Julien, *Les Français en Amérique*, extract, p. 31.
14) *Africa Pilot, vol I* (London: Hydrographic Department, 1953), pp. 54-59.
15) *Byron's Journal of his circumnavigation 1764-1766*, p. 17.
16) Julien, *Les Français en Amérique*, extract, pp. 31-32, note p. 32.
17) Julien, *Les Français en Amérique*, extract, p. 38.
18) Julien, *Les Français en Amérique*, extract, pp. 39-45.
19) d' Avezac, *Campagne du Navire l'Espoir*, p. 99. The men of *l'Espoir* were hailed as "anges descendus du ciel" by the Indians.
   Pierre Margry, *Les Navigations françaises et La révolution maritime du XIV au XVI siècles d'après les documents inédits tirés de France, d'Angleterre, d'Espagne et d'Italie* (Paris: Librairie Tross, 1867), p. 150.
   d'Avezac, *Campagne du Navire l'Espoir*, pp. 10-11.
20) Margry, *Navigations*, p. 141. Margry presented the itinerary which the abbé sent to Pope Alexander VII in its entirety.
21) Margry, *Navigations*, pp. 151-152.
22) Margry, *Navigations*, p. 153.
23) Margry, *Navigations*, p. 154.
   Early Voyages to Terre Australis now called Australia. ed. and

intro. by R. H. Major (New York: Burt Franklin, Hakluyt Society, ser. I, vol. 25), p. xviii.

24) Margry, *Navigations,* pp. 159-161.

25) d'Avezac, *Campagne du Navire l'Espoir,* pp. 38, 46-48, 50.

26) d'Avezac, *Campagne du Navire l'Espoir,* pp. 69-72.

27) Visconde de Porto Seguro (Varnhagen), *Historia Geral do Brasil* ... Vol. I (São Paulo-Cayeiras-Rio: Companhia Melhoramentos de São Paulo, Weizflog Irmaos Incorporada, 1935-36), p. 101.

CHAPTER V

ENTREPRENEURS & CORSAIRS

With ship and cargo at the bottom of the sea the only thing of value the surviving Normans took ashore was information. They knew that Brazil held rare products which could be sold at great profit. Shortly after the homecoming of the survivors of the *l'Espoir* adventure, three more Norman ships sailed to Brazil and entered the Paraguacu River. While the French were trading with the Indians, four Portuguese ships sailed in and discovered the uninvited guests. Before the sun set, two of the French ships were sunk and the crews killed. The few who managed to escape from the third ship fled in a long boat and were rescued by another French ship at Point Itapurama, about four leagues from Bahia.[1]

The beginnings of French commerce in Brazil had been cheerless but the Normans did not lose heart. The number of ships sent to Brazil increased. Many of them were owned or partly owned by an obstinate and imaginative merchant of Dieppe, Jean Ango.

Born in Dieppe in 1480, he was the son of a merchant who had risen from modest circumstances to a position of wealth and importance. Jean Ango the Elder was no ordinary merchant but an explorer as well, and his fleets often left the usual sailing routes to explore remote places. They were guided by serious students of navigation. In 1508, Jean Ango the Elder's ship *La*

Pensée, commanded by the pilot Thomas Aubert, cruised the waters of Newfoundland and the Canadian coast.[2]

The elder Ango endowed his son with a sound education. Young Ango received instruction in the classics, the arts, and the sciences. He learned mathematics and hydrography from the celebrated priest of Arques, Pierre Desceliers. Later in his life Jean Ango manifested his interest in the arts in his splendid wooden house on the quai in Dieppe. It was named *La Pensée* after his father's ship. Within it, Dieppe's own Medici placed works of the Italian Renaissance and met with his pilots. The deeds of brave Norman mariners were represented by bas-reliefs in the town house.

Jean Ango was an active and influential citizen of Dieppe. Before his career was over he had held nearly every important office in the area, many of them at the same time. He was counsellor of the village militia; tax collector; controller of the grain and salt stores; advisor to the governor of the city, then himself governor; recipient of the revenue from the temporal domains of Dieppe, Bouteilles and Pallet, of the Archbishopry of Rouen; Captain and Viscount of Dieppe, and Lieutenant de l'Amiral de France. He also was a favorite of Marguerite d'Angoulême, and in 1533 received Francis I at his château, Varengeville.[3]

To the Iberian monarchs, Manuel I and John III of Portugal, and the Emperor Charles V, Ango was a dangerous and disturbing enemy. He ranked among the most important shipowners of France. He built ships, he supplied fleets, and he was the villain behind the thieves who stole Spanish and Portuguese treasure at sea.

The thieves were among the brilliant scholars and mariners who surrounded Ango. They were: Pierre

Maucler, astronomer and mathematician; the brothers Raoul and Jean Parmentier, commanders of the first French expedition to the East Indies; Pierre Crignon, their poet-navigator companion; Jean Fleury, terror to Spanish and Portuguese mariners; Jehan Fain, Sylvestre Belles, and Jacques de Saint Maurice, all twice captured by the Portuguese, and Jean Verrazzano, the celebrated Florentine explorer.[4]

One of the more colorful of this illustrious group was Jean Fleury. After he seized the first treasure, including the king's fifth, sent by Hernando Cortés from Mexico, Charles V never forgot Jean Fleury. In 1523 the conqueror Cortés commissioned two officers, Alonso d'Avila and Antonio de Quiñones to deliver three ships filled with treasure valued at 130,000 castellanos to Spain. On board these ships were jaguars, vases, mitres, gold, silver, and an emerald "as large as the palm of the hand." Near the Azores out jumped Fleury with three nefs and five galleons, one of which, *Le Dieppe,* belonged to Ango. The Spaniards could not outrun Fleury. About ten leagues from Cape São Vicente, Fleury took two out of the three ships. Quiñones was fatally wounded in the furious battle. Later Cortés lamented to the Emperor that proper escort had not been provided by the Board of Trade:

> . . . I have learned that the articles which I transmitted to your imperial Majesty by the hands of Antonio de Quiñones and Alonso de Avila, the deputies from this New Spain, did not reach the royal presence, having been captured by the French in consequence of the little care taken by the Board of Trade at Seville in convoying them from the islands of the Azores . . .
>
> October 15, 1524, Temixitan[5]

In his *Opus Epistolarum,* decade VIII, Chapter II, Milan, 1530, Peter Martyr also reported the incident, as well as another earlier capture by the pirate from France. The first was a galleon sent from Santa Domingo laden with gold, sugar and other valuables:

> Ex Hispaniola, unionibus et auro, sacchareis que massis et cassia fistula navis nostris littoribus jam appropinquabat onustra. Pyrata Gallus, nomine Florinus in prospecto navis adortus, expugnavit ac cepit . . .

Jean Fleury did not limit his pillaging to Spanish vessels, but also removed cargo from Portuguese ships. The list submitted in a French-Portuguese reparations conference in 1539 was long. According to the Portuguese representative, Dr. Georgio Nunes, Fleury took his first Portuguese prize in August, 1521, when he stopped a ship sailing out of Lisbon. The Portuguese conjectured that Fleury's ship had been outfitted in Rouen. The next incident was in June, 1522 when Fleury with seven ships seized a Portuguese ship near Tenerife. Jean Ango was named the owner of the pirate ship. Next, in 1523, Fleury transshipped cargo valued at 180,000 ducats from a Portuguese vessel en route from the East Indies. In 1524, he met a ship returning from Brazil and not only emptied it but sank it. All hands were lost.[6]

Many in the Iberian peninsula were crying for revenge and a price was put on Fleury's head. In 1526, Jean Fleury wintered in Provence, then in the Spring of 1527 again took command of Ango's squadron. Soon he was back in his favorite hunting area near Cape São Vicente awaiting ships sailing for Spain and Portugal. This time his squadron of five ships was too spread out and he was challenged by a Basque captain, Martín Pérez de Irizar. Sails were ripped, castles blown away and Fleury was overcome. Knowing that he was a sought out man, Fleury offered the Basque 30,000 ducats for his release but was turned down. The Basque refused 10,000 ducats which the Portuguese offered for the pirate. From Cádiz, Magistrate Juan de Giles informed Charles V that Fleury was in the city under arrest. The Emperor granted full execution powers at once. Jean Fleury paid for his exploits with his life. On October 13, 1527, he and two of his lieutenants, Mezieres and Michel, were executed at Colmenar de Arenas. In gratitude to the Basque captain, Charles V granted him permission to add three "fleurs de lys" to his coat of arms. Some of the members of Fleury's crew were returned to France. Others, less fortunate, fell into the hands of Barbary pirates and were enslaved.[7]

Other corsairs were captured and their ships and goods were confiscated by the Spanish and Portuguese. Jehan Fain and Jacques de Saint-Maurice were twice imprisoned.[8] The first time they were in command of a ship owned by Jean Terrier, a Dieppe merchant and ship builder. He was also an author and wrote a small book describing how long voyages were financed.

According to *Le Guidon de la Mer,* two methods were used. The first, *au fret,* was simply a matter of the ship owners, *bourgeois de la nef,* supplying ships and goods and paying the captains and crews set sums for delivering freight to a specified place and bringing back goods received in exchange. The second and more commonly used method was *au tiers.* It was an effective way to disperse the great risk involved in sending a ship on a long voyage. As the term implies, the undertaking was considered in three parts: the ship, the crew, and the stores.

The ship and some or all of the arms to protect it were supplied by the *bourgeois de la nef.* He equipped the vessels with artillery, projectiles, harquebuses, lead, locks, powder, etc. He also provided things necessary for safe sailing such as lead, lines, compasses, clocks, and materials for repairs including tar, pitch, nails and pegs.

After the ship was built, the *bourgeois de la nef* appointed a master, and to sharpen his interest and performance, made him a part owner of the craft. He then chose a pilot, first mate, and crew. All hands met and decided what stores and equipment should be put aboard.

Sometimes the *bourgeois de la nef* paid for all stores and equipment himself, but more often, for long voyages the third party, the *victuailleurs,* was brought in. These merchants supplied materials for trade and victuals for the voyage, and if the *bourgeois de la nef* could not or would not provide all of the ship's equipment for the voyage, the master was sent to the various *victuailleurs* with a list of the things which were wanting. Those *victuailleurs* who were willing to increase their participation and risk in the voyage, signed for certain items, then advanced them. They were usually such things as powder, firepikes, and lances.

The rôle of the *victuailleurs* was highly speculative. Upon the return of the ship, if it returned, and if the voyage had been at all successful, the *victuailleurs* were paid one-third of the value of the goods they had advanced before the voyage. The other two-thirds went to the *bourgeois de la nef* and the crew. Then, and this was how a *victuailleur* might see his money grow, the profit from the voyage was divided three ways: owners, crews, suppliers. To a great extent, the *victuailleurs* gambled on the ability of the *bourgeois de la nef* to construct sound, fast ships, and the ability of the masters and crews to sail and defend them.

All three parties signed a contract which contained

the name of the ship, the names of all the people involved, the destination, the date of departure, and the
interest rate of the borrowed money involved.[9]

Another author of Dieppe was Pierre Crignon, stu-
dent of astrology and cosmography, pilot and poet. His
songs were often sung at fêtes in Dieppe and Rouen.
In 1531, he published the works of Jean Parmentier
who had died en route from Sumatra. In 1534 he wrote
a treatise on the variations of the compass and dedicated
it to Philip Chabot, Admiral of France. He also had a
great deal to say on freedom of the seas, a favorite
subject of French citizens on land or sea. From the
moment a ship sailed out of home port, all hands were
in grave danger. But this was true of all sailors from all
places and accepted. What was not accepted was that
there were few places on the great and wide sea that the
French could frequent without being accused of entering
someone else's private waters, and being treated as
pirates, pests, interlopers, and criminals. The French
felt slighted and did not for a moment hesitate to assume
the role assigned to them—that of the underdog. Pierre
Crignon had this to say:

> Even though the Portuguese are the tiniest nation on the
> earth, it apparently is not large enough to satisfy their lust.
> They would have to drink the dust of King Alexander's
> heart to demonstrate such excessive ambition. They think
> that they hold in one hand something which they could not
> embrace with both, and it seems that God made the seas
> for them and that other nations are not worthy of sailing on
> them. Surely, if it were possible for them to close the seas
> from Cape Finisterre to Ireland, they would have done it a
> long time ago. Just as the Portuguese do not have the right
> to prevent French trade in the lands they presumptuously
> claim, and in which they are neither loved nor obeyed, we
> do not possess the right to keep them from calling at Scot-
> land, Denmark, or Norway, even though we were there first.[10]

58   REGINA JOHNSON TOMLINSON

NOTES

1) Varnhagen, *Historia Geral*, pp. 119, 412. Varnhagen cites "Enformação do Brasil e de suas capitanias, 1584."

Eugène Guénin, *Ango et ses pilots d'après documents inédits tirées des archives de France, de Portugal, et d'Espagne* (Paris: Imprimerie Nationale, 1901), p. 4. Guénin cites the same source.

Gaffarel, *Histoire du Brésil Français au seizième siècle*, p. 91.

2) Gaffarel, *Brésil Français*, pp. 55-56.

3) La Roncière, *Marine Française*, pp. 243-246.

Guénin, *Ango*, pp. 1-5.

Lavisse, *Histoire de France*, V, I, p. 279.

4) Gaffarel, *Brésil Français*, pp. 60-62.

Guénin, *Ango*, pp. 1-11.

5) La Roncière, *Marine française*, pp. 249-250.

Guénin, *Ango*, pp. 18-24, cites Herrera, Decade iii, VI, lib. III, and Peter Martyr, Letter from Valladolid, June 11, 1523" OPUS EPISTOLARUM, Milan, 1530, letter 735.

The Despatches of Hernando Cortes, the conqueror of Mexico addressed to the Emperor Charles V written during the conquest and containing a narrative of its events. Intro. and notes by George Folsom (New York: Wiley and Putnam, 1843), p. 421.

6) Guénin, *Ango*, pp. 30-41, The records of the "réclamations rédigées" by Dr. Georgio Nunes representative of Portugal, of John III, and official delegate to the "Tribunal des Prises" at Bayonne are quoted in part by Guénin. The original records are in the Torre do Tombo in Lisbon.

7) Guénin, *Ango*, pp. 52-58, 243-248. Correspondence between Chas. V, licentiates Herrera and Juan de Giles, and Corregidor di Xeres, dated 11 Oct. to 27 Nov., 1527.

La Ronciere, *Marine Française*, III, pp. 252-254.

Julien, *Voyages de découverte*, p. 98.

8) Both incidents led to the requesting and granting of Letters of Marque.

9) Guénin, *Ango*, pp. 67-71.

Charles and Paul Bréard, *Documents relatifs à la Marine Normande et ses armements aux XVIe et XVIIe siècles pour le Canada, l'Afrique, les Antilles, le Brésil, et les Indes, recueillis annotés et publiés par Charles et Paul Bréard.* (Rouen: A Lestringant, 1889), pp. 11-12. Chapter 11, *Le Guidon de la Mer.*

10) Guénin, *Ango*, p. 12.

CHAPTER VI

STRUGGLE

Just as Pierre Crignon wrote, no one questioned the right of the Portuguese to call at the ports of established kingdoms such as Denmark or Norway. The disagreement, rather, was over new ports and places. Portugal, now the owner of a new empire which sprawled from the Moluccas to Africa to Brazil, had a colossal problem in her pocket. How would she control her real estate? Various monarchs tried various ways. In 1504 Manuel I forbade his subjects to sell maps or globes which indicated the positions of countries south of the islands of São Tomé, Del Principe and the mouth of the Rio Manicongo. Even though all three were in the Atlantic Ocean, this meant, roughly, anything, anywhere south of the equator. In order to limit knowledge about Portuguese places to Portuguese heads, Don Manuel attempted to prevent his captains from hiring foreign crews or pilots.[1]

The crown soon perceived that the area was too large, and the people within it too many for efficient control, and changed its approach to the problem. Don Manuel decided better to limit Portuguese activities within the empire. In Brazil, his subjects were ordered to limit themselves to the area between the Rivers Amazon and

Plate. In 1516, Don Manuel drew up tentative plans for colonization including the formation of captaincies of sea and land. But still the area was too large for effective patrol, and the Breton and Norman interlopers continued to enter and trade. The conflict between the Portuguese and the interlopers soon developed into a small but authentic war between France and Portugal.[2]

In 1521, Manuel I "The Fortunate" died and John III, "The Pious" ascended the throne. He firmly believed that the Portuguese monopoly in Brazil was both sacred and legitimate. The bishops of Rome had proclaimed it; Spain had agreed to it. When the distasteful news reached Lisbon that Francis I had implied approval of a discovery expedition to the Orient and a project to plant Frenchmen in Brazil, John III determined to take action. He dispatched an ambassador, João da Silveira, to France with instructions to prevent the expedition, demand compensation for lost ships, and request a formal guarantee that French attacks on Portuguese ships cease. The ambassador was at liberty to declare that the French would suffer both financially and physically if they did not heed the warning. Also included in the message was that John III was quite aware that France and Portugal were not at war and were good friends, and that this was why he had discouraged the unofficial war in his own kingdom. The Portuguese monarch suggested that restitution be made by French and Portuguese alike, and that justice be done.[3]

John III felt that the time was right for negotiations. French ambitions had grown to dangerous proportions. Perhaps he was willing to make concessions, but there is no evidence that he intended to cease treating the French interlopers as anything but pests and pirates, which from his position is exactly what they were. As negotiations continued, measures for discouraging the French traders continued. In fact, the negotiations proved nothing. The French voyages had sprung up locally and were privately directed. The king had very little to say or do about them and certainly was not in a position to dictate policy on this matter. Moreover, perhaps he did not wish to. His position was hardly enviable. He was off and on at war with Charles V. He was involved in Italy. He sought good will with Portugal, even instigated negotiations for the marriage of his daughter, Charlotte, to John III. But he did not at this point seriously interfere with the activities of the interlopers. He could hardly approve of snuffing out their trading and at the same time expect them to assist him in his struggle with the Hapsburgs. Men like Jean Ango were aware of this and of the value of gifts at court too. Those who understood his problems and aided him were well rewarded with wealth and rare things many of which had been removed from Portuguese ships.[4]

Before long the official negotiations were broken down by the unofficial war. Individuals, kings included, took recourse to the most expedient methods for reimbursement, and when possible, gathered a little extra too. Anger and revenge only intensified the economic war at sea. One of the first incidents which caused the French to set their sails for more plundering and revenge occurred in 1522. Jean Terrier had outfitted a ship for battle against Charles V, and Captain Jehan Fain had gone about boarding and looting Spanish ships, then sailed to Portugal to put his prisoners ashore there. When he reached Portuguese waters, Pedro Botelho, commander of the Portuguese fleet arrested him and his crew and confiscated their loot and ship. Fain and his crew spent five months in prison.[5]

The men of Dieppe, not about to accept this sort of treatment in silence, applied to the French court for permission to revenge the Portuguese insolence. In September, 1522, Jean Terrier was granted a Letter of Marque from the Admiral of France, Guillaume Gonffier, Lord of Bonivet. It stated that Fain and his crew had been unjustly treated and that Terrier was authorized recourse to his own means to regain prisoners, ship and cargo.[6] That was sufficient encouragement for other Frenchmen who were seething with bitter feelings. They did not await official authorization. In 1526 in Rio São Francisco in Brazil three French vessels met the Portuguese ship São Gabriel. At first it seemed that the mariners far from home had forgotten the unofficial war. The Portuguese sent a long boat to the French not only with a pilot to guide them up the river but caulking compound for repairs. The good will was short lived. A minor scuffle among the sailors soon grew into a serious battle. French cannon ball ripped through the São Gabriel and her captain, Rodrigo d'Acunha, was taken prisoner.[7]

John III was exasperated. Negotiations hardly mattered now. The French army had been crushed at the battle of Pavia; Francis I had been imprisoned in Spain and had signed the humiliating Treaty of Madrid. John III took action and ordered Christovão Jaques to take a squadron to the coast of Brazil and destroy every French person and establishment he found. Jaques executed his mission with extraordinary zeal. At Bahia, his swift lateen-riggers met three ships being loaded with Brazilwood. In the surprise attack the Breton pilots and most of the crew died. Some survivors managed to get ashore. Others, some 300 men, were taken to Pernambuco where they were hanged or buried to their shoulders and used as targets for harquebus practice. Jacques continued his pest extermination as far as Río de Janeiro attacking ships, destroying establishments, and raiding Indians who were allied with the French.[8]

Normans and Bretons objected. They insisted that they were engaged in commerce not piracy, and began to refer to treaties for proof. They were quick to remind the Portuguese (and French court) that in 1469 a treaty had been signed stating that Bretons could freely trade with Portugal and her possessions, and that it had been reaffirmed by Kings Charles VIII and John II, then stating that the subjects of France and Portugal could trade in the possessions of both kingdoms. But, in fact, no one was minding treaties any more.[9] John III was concerned about the control of his empire, and Francis I was preoccupied with arrangements for the release of his sons who were now imprisoned in his stead. Two French agents were sent to Lisbon. One was instructed to obtain indemnity for the families of the victims of the Bahia slaughter; the other was to attempt to procure a loan of 400,000 cruzados for part of the ransom Charles V demanded for the release of the King of France's sons. Francis I actually was quite willing to forget the complaints of French mariners in order to regain the royal prisoners, and suggested that a tribunal settle reclamations and agree on a zone where the French could safely sail. John III did not hesitate to take advantage of an advantageous situation. He instructed his ambassador, da Silveira, to promise Francis I 100,000 cruzados. The other 300,000 cruzados, he suggested, be taken from the funds the French owed the Portuguese, and estimated that this was 300 ships and 500,000 cruzados.[10] John III further suggested that the French cease seizing Portuguese ships whether at war with another nation or not. This implied that the Portuguese could, if they wished, assist the Spanish in their war with France. John III would not hear of a safe zone and repeated that the French were not welcomed in any Portuguese territory. Francis I did not object. He was in no position to argue, or not until he had raised the ransom for the release of his sons. When he did this, he dismissed John III's demands as unreasonable.[11]

At the French court, the entrepreneurs and their spokesmen complained. Now the focal point was a ship from Dieppe, *La Marie.* After removing cargo from Spanish galleons, she had been blown to the Portuguese coast, then captured, and with cargo, confiscated. The captain, the same Jehan Fain, master and crew were condemned to death. The French argued that the cargo was Spanish or perhaps American and that the Portuguese were not justified in seizing it from the French. There was no word as to whether the French were justified in their seizures. Eventually, the cargo was kept, and the prisoners were pardoned and turned over to the French ambassador, Honoré de Caix. Upon reaching France, the mariners insisted that they had been victims of fraud.[12]

In August, 1529, Jean Ango and the Vice-Admiral of France, Charles de Bec determined to recover the loss at their own expense. When Portuguese ships were seized, the cost of the project was to be deducted, and the remainder divided in half. One half was to go to Ango and Charles de Bec, the other to the owners of *La Marie,* the Morel brothers. Jean Ango did not possess a Letter of Marque granting him to secure reimbursement by his own devices, but he did have a friend at court, Philip Chabot, now Admiral of France. In exchange for a Letter of Marque, Chabot received a "magnificent diamond." Even the king's sister took an interest in Ango's problems and wrote a letter to the Chancellor of France, Antoine de Prat, which suggested that the loyal Viscount of Dieppe be granted his request.[13]

Ango's Letter of Marque expressed the sentiments of many Normans. It said that it had been granted because so many Normans and Bretons had suffered at the hands of the Portuguese and that Frenchmen had rights to sail the seas and to seek reparations for damages. If reparations were not forthcoming, then Ango and company were authorized to seize them up to the amount of 250,000 and 10,000 ducats.[14]

That was clear enough. Portuguese agents in France immediately began to gather all possible information on Ango's plans for reprisal. One agent, Gaspard Palha, who had replaced the late da Silveira, wrote John III that Ango did not have a ship in the water. Some speculated that Ango would seek revenge in Malaguette or somewhere else in African waters. Palha reported that Ango had procured one orange-laden caravel in Rouen and a hooker filled with merchandise for His Majesty in Brittany. Rumor whispered. that Ango was preparing a fleet to sail for Madeira.[15]

As for Jean Ango himself, he intended to seize Portuguese cargo in the Atlantic and close the route to Flanders. But the unlucky viscount was not to possess his Letter of Marque long enough to do any substantial damage to Portuguese shipping, or for that matter, to collect total reparations for the loss of *La Marie*.

The Portuguese were quick to realize that the Letter of Marque was a declaration of war against Portuguese commerce, and that the obvious solution was to have it revoked.[16] An extraordinary envoy, Don Antonio de Ataïde, was sent to Francis I with instructions to register complaint about Ango's bellicose gestures and request the revocation of the Letter of Marque. Should the French court refuse the request, de Ataïde was ordered to purchase the Letter of Marque.

Antonio de Ataïde arrived in París on April 22, 1531. Two days later his assistant, Jayne de Bregence, wrote John III suggesting that he turn to Charles V for assistance. Charles V was receptive and soon intervened in John III's favor. He sent his own extraordinary envoy with letters for Francis I, the queen (Charles V's sister, Eleonore), and other powerful people. Meanwhile, John III and his agents had prepared the ground for bribery.[17]

Philip Chabot, Admiral of France, was cooperative. In return for 25,000 escuz, a tapestry worth 10,000 escuz and 16,000 francs, he promised to prevent French ships from going to Malaguette and Brazil.[18] John III offered Jean Ango 60,000 francs for reparations and his agents arranged a meeting with the viscount. On July 11, 1531 at Fontainebleau, Ango agreed to surrender the hard sought Letter of Marque.[19]

Ango had little choice but to accept the 60,000 francs. When the Portuguese envoy had first approached Francis I with the request that Ango be stopped, the king had been non-commital, then stated that it was Ango not the king who was making war. The envoy was referred to the Council, and Ango was forced to defend his Letter of Marque. Meanwhile, Charles V in an effort to calm the corsairs, released several of Fleury's companions on June 30, 1531.[20] The Council did not revoke Ango's letter and he sent a fleet to the Azores to seize Portuguese shipping. John III then issued definite orders to purchase the Letter of Marque and Philip Chabot then sold it. Ango realized if the Admiral of France was willing to accept "gifts" from the Portuguese, there was little he could do to retain support from the court. He decided to officially relent and accepted the 60,000 francs.

The not so honorable Admiral of France attempted to honor his part of the agreement and published announcements in Picardy and Norman ports which forbade trade in Brazil or Malaguette. Shipowners protested that Ango had no reason to obey anyone in the service of the King of Portugal, and turned to the Admiralty for aid, but Chabot was too powerful.[21] On November 20, 1531, he issued the official order which forbade all ships prepared for voyages to Brazil or Guinea to sail.[22]

Reliable evidence on how the corsairs reacted to the embargo is lacking, but there is reason to believe that the French had no respect for Chabot's announcements and continued with their trading in Portuguese territories. Seven years later at a conference in Bayonne, evidence was presented that the French had attempted to establish a factory in Brazil. Thus, Normans and Bretons were not idle after 1531 and the Chabot episode.[23]

While kings, envoys and agents had been negotiating, a small group of Frenchmen had been struggling to establish a foothold in Brazil. The entrepreneur, Bertrand d'Ornesan, Baron de Saint Blanchard, had hoped to found a settlement which would serve as a warehouse and point of coordination between French traders and Brazilian Indians. In 1530, with the permission of Francis I, the ship, La Pelerine, commanded by Jean Duperet, set sail from Marseille. On board were 120 men and arms for the defense of the ship and the factory in Brazil. After three months at sea the ship landed at Pernambuco where it was greeted by an attack of Indians and Portuguese. But the French had come prepared and won the battle. After a truce was made the French hired the Portuguese to aid them in rebutting further attacks from the Indians, and trading was begun. When *La Pelerine* was filled with goods, she returned to Europe for more supplies. In August, 1531, she put in at Málaga. When six Portuguese caravels appeared with offers of ship's biscuit and escort, the French for some reason, accepted. En route to Marseille, the fleet was becalmed, and the Portuguese signaled for the French officers to board their flagship. Again, the French accepted. The officers were seized, the cargo was pillaged, and the French and information about the factory in Brazil were forthwith delivered to the King of Portugal. Another Portuguese extermination expedition was prepared for Brazil. In December, 1531, Pedro Lopez, with three ships in his command, set sail for Pernambuco. Lopez besieged the French factory for 18 days at which time the French commander, M. de la Motte, requested that peace talks be started. It was agreed that the Portuguese would possess the fort and that the French would be delivered to free territory, but on surrendering, M. de la Motte and twenty others were hanged. Several were awarded to the Indians for their cannibalistic festivals. The remainder were taken to Portugal, imprisoned, and according to Baron de Saint Blanchard's report at the 1538 Bayonne conference, maltreated and forced to sign false declarations.[23]

The Portuguese attempts to stop the interlopers, the methods of John III and his pensioners in France, and the very financial necessity to continue trading drove the French to more activity and more furious plundering. Francis I was of no help. It seemed that his vacillating from one policy to another would never cease. Jean Ango pitted himself against the King of Portugal.[24]

The Portuguese monarch turned to a new approach

and suggested the marriage of his half sister Maria to the Dauphin. As far as Francis I was concerned much of the success of this project depended upon the importation of spices into France. John III expressed willingness to review the possibility of 2,000 to 4,000 cruzados per annum of pepper, and perhaps ginger too, if something were done about the incorrigible French pests who roamed Portuguese waters.

With the approaching 1536-38 Valois-Hapsburg conflict, Francis I was prepared to go to some length for the friendship of Portugal, even at the expense of French commerce. Charles V was also anxious for Portuguese cooperation. For the moment, John III decided that he had more to gain from France. He feared the power of the Hapsburg empire and needed help to keep the Flanders spice route open. And there was always the possibility that the corsairs would somehow be brought under control. Both the Portuguese and French courts declared that they wished to bravely fight piracy, but as before, this desire got little beyond its being uttered.

On July 14, 1536, France and Portugal signed a treaty of cooperation at Lyons. Ports and roadsteads of both kingdoms were to be "free and common to their subjects" and cargo was to be "received in safety." "Freedom of commerce" was one of the objects of the treaty; friends of the kingdoms of Portugal and France were to carry certificates stating this.

As Spanish ships and cargo could be confiscated, the Portuguese were cautioned not to use Spanish ships or carry Spanish goods. The French were permitted to take booty from the high seas into Portuguese ports, but they were never to seize ships belonging to the friends of the King of France. Sailing into Portuguese waters did not mean seizing Portuguese shipping. Likewise the Portuguese were not to harm the friends of their king. Those who took liberties would be punished as violators of the peace.[26]

The following month Letters-Patent from Francis I were delivered to his governors, admirals, judges and other authorities. They stated that violators would be punished and booty would be returned. In May of the next year, French ships were again forbidden to sail to the coasts of Malaguette, Brazil or any other Portuguese place. Those who did not comply would receive corporal punishment, and their ships and goods would be confiscated. The Letters-Patent were renewed in August, 1537, September-December, 1538, and January, 1539.[27]

The interlopers were bitter and felt slighted. Again, their spokesman, Pierre Crignon, expressed their collective indignation, "If the king would release the check on French traders, in less than four or five years, they would win for him the friendship and assured obedience of Brazilian natives with no arms except persuasion and good conduct."[28] This friendship was of great importance to the Norman and Breton interlopers. Shipowners and mariners had too much at stake. They could not obey an order they could not justify. Their voyages to Brazil continued, and John III continued to object to them.[29]

Protests from both French and Portuguese shippers and officials led to an exchange of letters and eventually to the conference held in May, 1539 at Bayonne. Dr. Georgio Nunes, the Portuguese representative, enumerated French incidents, mostly those of the late Jean Fleury. He suggested that Fleury's son, François, pay for the extensive damage wrought by his father. French complaints were mostly presented by two investors who had lost a great deal: the Baron de Saint Blanchard and the Viscount of Dieppe. Jean Ango's claims were for payment for ships and cargo lost to the Portuguese. He based his argument on the 1536 Lyons Treaty and attempted to remind the Portuguese that they had no right to seize friendly ships which had been sent out to attack Spanish vessels. He inquired about the "freedom of commerce" which both France and Portugal had supported, but soon discovered that it was not quite as he had wished. He received no compensation. Later, in February 1544, Ango was granted a new Letter of Marque which authorized him to seize what he was not able to obtain at Bayonne.[30]

The plundering, the private revenge continued, but the attitude of the crown changed. The French court began to show an interest in exploration and colonization. Others soon took note. Charles V was not pleased by Jacques Cartier's third voyage. The diplomats again applied themselves and a treaty was drawn up and signed by France and Spain at Crépy-en-Laonnais on September 18, 1544. Charles V's immediate goal was to bring to a halt French plundering of Caribbean settlements. In return for suspending these raids, French subjects were granted permission to trade in the Indies.[31]

The treaty was never ratified. When it was drawn up there was an outcry to the Council of the Indies. Iberians considered the French as nothing more than knaves and pirates. The King of Portugal insisted that the treaty was harmful to Portuguese and Spanish interests as now the French could simply go on plundering in exclusive Portuguese and Spanish waters but at less risk. He added that it was impossible to patrol that amount of sea and coast line. The King of France again cooperated. Just before his death, Francis I agreed to suspend the Letters of Marque and forbade his subjects from voyaging to the overseas possessions of Spain.[32]

Again, the French corsairs were illegal and without an ally. Again, they attempted to cause the King of Portugal to pay dearly for trying to close the sea or at least to partition it. On May 12, 1548, John III issued a statement to his captaincies on the need for defense against the French vultures. In December of the next year, Henry II of France reaffirmed his father's act of February 28, 1547, and suspended all Letters of Marque for ten years.

The corsairs were defenseless against their own government. Continually the crown had used the Letters of Marque for diplomatic gymnastics, not for the protection of French commerce. When the king wished to express displeasure with Portuguese policy, he granted the Letters of Marque. When he approved or sought a change of policy, he cancelled the Letters of Marque.[33]

The result was that the merchants, mariners and entrepreneurs, Ango among them, suffered. With no consistant cooperation from the crown, with some of its more powerful personalities in outright collaboration with the enemy, with no legal recourse, great amounts of wealth constantly dwindled away. In an almost superhuman effort to save himself from ruin, Ango took charge of naval operations against the English. In 1545, he organized a large expedition against them, but the Royal Treasury did not reimburse him for the costly expedition. The viscount then retired to his château in Dieppe where he devoted the rest of his days trying to keep the rest of his fortune from his relentless creditors. Had the king not eventually intervened, he would have been imprisoned.[34]

Many of the entrepreneurs went into bankruptcy.

Ango was not alone. One thing was certain and obvious. Long voyages were risky and all too often the original investment was not recovered. The intense interest in trading in Brazil, and the willingness to risk capital and life soon declined.[35]

NOTES

1) Gaffarel, *Brésil Français*, pp. 89-90.

   Morison, *Portuguese Voyages*, p. 77, His source is *Alguns Documentos do Archivo Nacional da Torre do Tombo acerca das navegaçoes e conquistas portuguezas*, ed. Jose Ramos-Coelho (Lisboa: 1894), p. 139.

2) Julien, *Voyages de découverte*, pp. 91-92.

3) Julien, *Voyages de découverte*, p. 93, The instructions were probably issued by Antonio Carneiro, secr. of state, ft. n.

   Guénin, *Ango*, p. 80, Letter from João da Silveira to John III, Dec. 24, 1521, and pp. 187-190, M. de Santarem, *Quadro elementar das relaçoes politicas e diplomaticas de Portugal con as diversas potencias do mundo, taken from originals in the Torre do Tombo*.

4) Julien, *Voyages de découverte*, p. 94.

5) Guénin, *Ango*, pp. 67 and 71.

6) Guénin, *Ango*, p. 47, Letter of Marque to Jean Terrier from Francis I, Sept. 3, 1522. (Bibliothéque Nationale, MSS. port. de Fontette No. 11) Jean Fleury was given the task of recovering the value of the confiscated cargo.

7) La Roncière, *Marine Française*, p. 279.

8) Guénin, *Ango*, p. 29.

   La Roncière, *Marine Française*, p. 279.

   Julien, *Voyages de découverte*, pp. 95-96.

   Gafferal, *Brésil Français*, p. 95.

9) Julien, *Voyages de découverte*, p. 96.

   E. Gomes de Carvalho, *D. João III e os Franceses* (Lisbon: Teixera, 1909), pp. 20-21.

10) Guénin, *Ango*, p. 193, Letter from John III to João da Silveira, 26 Jan., 1530.

    Julien, *Voyages de découverte*, pp. 96-97.

11) Julien, *Voyages de découverte,* p. 98.

12) Guénin, *Ango,* pp. 72-73.
Julien, *Voyages de découverte,* pp. 98-99.

13) Guénin, *Ango,* pp. 88-89. Letter from Marguerite to Antoine de Prat, June 10, 1530, Blois.

14) Guénin, *Ango,* pp. 194, 249-254, Letter of Marque dated July 27, 1530, Bibliothèque National, MSS Français, registre répertoire No. 5503, fol. 58 Vo. Lettre de Marque contre les Portugaloys. Also in Torre do Tombo — Gaveta 3, maco 1, No. 19.

15) Guénin, *Ango,* pp. 90-91. Malaguette (or maniguette) today is the name for a kind of pepper from Guinea, also called Guinea pepper.

16) Julien, *Voyages de découverte,* p. 106.

17) Guénin, *Ango,* pp. 92-101. All the letters are given.

18) Guénin, *Ango,* p. 103. "L'Acte d'accusation de l'Amiral."
Julien, *Voyages de découverte,* p. 107.

19) Guénin, *Ango,* p. 104, By an act drawn up before the notaries in Rouen, Feb. 20, 1532, Ango recognized the sum from Antonio Ataide and remitted the Letter of Marque.

20) Guénin, *Ango,* pp. 101-103.
La Roncière, *Marine Française,* p. 284.

21) Guénin, *Ango,* pp. 196-197. Letter from Doctor Gaspar Vez, Ambassador from Portugal to France written to John III.

22) Guénin, *Ango,* pp. 197-198, The Portuguese suggested that French ships also be prevented from voyaging to the Cape Verde Islands.

23) Guénin, *Ango,* pp. 256-261 (in Latin), pp. 43-46 (in French) "La Protestation de Bertrand d'Ornesan, Baron de Saint-Blanchard, contre la prise de la Pelerine, remise ... à Bayonne" at the conference at Bayonne, March 11, 1538. The document includes the story of the French efforts to establish a factory in Brazil.
For a list of the goods on board *La Pelerine,* see same book and chapter VII, footnote 1 of this book.

24) Guénin, *Ango,* p. 145.
Julien, *Voyages de découverte,* p. 131, from Carvalho, *D. João III e os Franceses,* p. 75.

25) Julien, *Voyages de découverte,* pp. 132-133.
Davenport, *European Treaties,* p. 199.

26) Guénin, *Ango,* pp. 201-202, the treaty is also in Davenport, *European Treaties,* pp. 201-204.

27) Guénin, *Ango,* pp. 202-205, Lettres Patent are given in La Roncière, *Marine Française III,* p. 292. His sources are British Museum ms. Cotton, Nero B 1, fol. 69, 102, Gaffarel, "Jean Ango" in Le Bulletin de la Societé Normande de geographie, 1889, m. 250.

Julien, *Voyages de découverte,* p. 134.

28) Julien, *Voyages de découverte,* p. 134.

La Roncière, *Marine Française, III,* p. 236.

29) Julien, *Voyages de découverte,* p. 135, ft. n. Commission du 2 juin, 1537, donnée par François I à Jean de Calvimont, second president et à Bertrand de Moncaupt, conseiller au parlement de Bordeaux, d'enquêter sur les faits et procéder si necessaire contre les coupables, in Guénin, *Ango,* pp. 205-206.

30) Guénin, *Ango,* pp. 31, 208 (letters leading up to the conference, reports of lawyers), 82-84 (for the names of ships which Ango lost-Acts of the Parliament of Rouen). On freedom of the seas pp. 46-47.

p. 42 concerns the Feb. 3, 1544 Letter of Marque. Ango was especially interested in gaining satisfaction for the three ships —*La Michelle, La Musette,* and *L'Allouette.* Letters of Francis I on Ango's losses are pp. 148-155.

31) Davenport, *European Treaties,* pp. 206 and 209.

Julien, *Voyages de découverte,* p. 170.

32) Davenport, *European Treaties,* p. 207.

La Roncière, *Marine Française,* III, 302-303.

Julien, *Voyages de découverte,* pp. 170-171.

Guénin, *Ango,* p. 233, February 28, 1547, the King of France agreed to suspend all Letters of Marque for two years if the King of Portugal would do the same.

33) Guénin, *Ango,* pp. 233-235.

Julien, *Voyages de découverte,* p. 172.

34) La Roncière, *Marine Française,* III, pp. 305-306.

Guénin, *Ango,* pp. 163-164, Actes de tabellionage, Rouen state transactions between Robert Michel, a merchant who loaned Ango supplies, and butchers who loaned him victuals. There are records of other loans to Ango.

35) Guénin, *Ango,* p. 165.

CHAPTER VII

IN BRAZIL

While they traded in Brazil, the French learned about that new land and the people who inhabited it, and soon knew a great deal about the languages and ways of life of the Indians. Some Frenchmen conformed to Indian customs in order to establish better trade relations, others because they preferred their manner of living.

For trade with the Brazilians, the French sent guns and powder, knives, hatchets, mirrors, combs, scissors, beads and other trinkets. In exchange, they received Brazilwood, cotton, feathers, skins, monkeys, parrots, humming birds, gold, grain, and medicines. The Brazilwood was cut down so rapidly that the Indians were forced to seek more in the interior. Feathers became fashionable in Europe and soon adorned ladies and gentlemen at court. Parrots were in demand and squirrel monkeys were soon favorite pets. As they did not long survive, they had to be frequently replaced by more from Brazil.[1]

The society the French encountered in Brazil was a simple one. The Indians lived from hand to mouth on millet, beans, turnips, fish, rabbits, ducks, geese, and chickens. They drank a sort of beer, probably made millet, which often intoxicated them. They had no schedule for meals, but ate when they were hungry. Their daughters were quickly entrusted to the foreigners, but their wives lived only with their husbands.[2]

Some of the Indians practiced cannibalism. This did not go unnoticed by Michel de Montaigne who in his celebrated essay "Of Cannibals" endeavored to point out to supposedly civilized people that cannibalism did not necessarily mean barbarism, and that for the Indians it was a test of bravery and dignity. As to prisoners who were taken in battle Montaigne wrote:

> These prisoners are so far from submitting in spite of all that is done to them that . . . during the two or three months they are kept, they bear a cheerful countenance; they urge their masters to make haste to bring them to the test; they defy them, rail at them, and reproach them with cowardice and the number of battles they have lost against those of their country. I have a song composed by a prisoner in which there is this thrust, that they come boldly, all of them, and assemble to dine upon him, for they will be eating at the same time their own fathers and grandfathers, whose flesh has served to feed and nourish his body. 'These muscles,' says he, 'this flesh and these veins are your own, poor fools that you are. You do not recognize that the substance of your ancestors' limbs is here yet; savor them well, and you will find in them taste of your own flesh.' An idea that does not smack at all of barbarity. Those that paint these people dying and reproduce the execution depict the prisoner spitting in the face of his executioners and making faces at them. In truth, to the very last gasp they never cease to brave and defy them both by word and gesture. In plain truth, here are men who are real savages in comparison with us; for either they must be absolutely so, or else we are savages; there is an amazing difference in their character and ours.[3]

Montaigne claimed to have talked with a savage in Rouen.

These were the Indians the French studied. Often they left young men ashore to learn Indian languages and make arrangements for the exchange of goods. Sometimes these men jumped ship and permanently joined the natives.[4]

One of the best testimonies to the presence of the French in Brazil and their trading activities is an account by a Hessian, Hans Stade. In search for adventure, of which he found an abundance, Hans went to Brazil twice, first with the Portuguese, later with the Spanish. His story is laced with almost comical frantic cries to heaven for freedom from his hungry captors. He was in Brazil about eight years. For some nine months he was a prisoner of the Tupinambá Indians. His description was, "They live in America; their country is situated in 24 degrees on the south side of the equinoctial line, and their country is bounded by a river called Rio de Jenero." Not long after his arrival in Brazil, Hans, to his extreme discomfort, became entangled in the political scene.

Years before, when Manuel had grasped the potential of Brazil and had realized that he could not patrol or protect so lengthy a coast line, he had drawn limits to official Portuguese activities. They were at the estuaries of the Amazon and Plata rivers. In 1516 rough plans for colonization were drawn up. The heart of Portuguese activity was on the island of San Vicente and Santa Amare, and on the mainland at Brikoika where a fort was built. The French usually frequented Saint Augustine and Port Royal farther north. Hans' wretched nine months were at least partially brought about by the Indians' involvement in French-Portuguese competition. The allies of the Portuguese were the Tupinikin Indians. North of them were the friends of the French, the Tupinambás.[5]

On his second visit to Brazil in 1540, Hans was a passenger on a Spanish ship from Seville. The ship called at

Lisbon, the Canary Islands, Guines and São Tomé. On São Tomé, Hans wrote, "rich in sugar, but unhealthy" and that the Portuguese lived there with black Moorish slaves. After leaving São Tomé, Hans' ship lost her companion vessels and became thrown off course for four months by contrary winds. Then in September, "the winds began to be northerly, and we directed our course south-south-west towards America." At Latitude S. 28°, after six months at sea, the voyagers not only found land but ran aground on it.

Through a series of events, Hans was drawn into the service of the Portuguese. When they discovered he was Hessian and well versed in artillery, they offered him an attractive salary to remain on the Island of Santa Amero, and direct the completion of the fort there. He finished the fort and requested leave but was persuaded to remain another two years. He also received a "privilegea," his commission as a gunner.

Hans had companionship in another German named Heliodorus. He was the manager of a sugar mill on the Island of San Vicente just five miles away. Hans also had a slave whom he sent out for hunting. One day as Hans was walking through the woods to pick up the game which the slave had killed he was captured by the Tupinambá Indians and carried off to a settlement called Ubatuba. The Indians discussed killing Hans immediately, but decided better to drag him home so that their wives could meet him and then dine on him. The Indians believed that Hans was Portuguese and they did not want to arouse the Portuguese fort at Brikioka. The unfortunate Hessian knew that these Indians were friends of the French. There was proof in the French guns and powder which his captors carried. If only he could convince them that he was French! For a moment they believed him.

After all, he declared, he had a red beard, and men from Portugal had black ones.

During his sojourn with the Tupinambás, one of Hans' happiest days was when he heard that a Frenchman was trading just a few miles away. When the Frenchman arrived at the village, Hans hoped that he would help to convince the Indians that Hans was friend not foe. Unfortunately Hans did not understand his would-be-liberator's French well enough to convince him that he was not Portugucsc, but he did understand the Indians language well enough to realize that the French trader reported that Hans was an enemy of the French and Indians, and advised that he be eaten at once. Later, when plans were being made to devour Hans, he was reminded that he had been quite unable to converse with the "chief's son." Meanwhile Hans had been singing the hymn "Now beg we of the Holy Ghost, The true belief we wish for most, That He may save us at our end, When from this vale of tears we wend." At that the Indians cried, "He is true Portuguese, now he howls, he dreads death."

Some weeks later the French trader, Karwattu Ware, returned. Again he visited Hans, but this time they conversed in the language of the Indians. Hans told him the whole story of coming over with the Spaniards, of his shipwreck, of working for the Portuguese. The Frenchman apologized for his error and swore "that he had believed (Hans) to be no other than one of the Portuguese, who were such great villains, that if they were ever to catch any of them in that province of Brazil they would hang them at once which is true; also, said he, that they had to give way to the savages, and were obliged to be satisfied with the manner in which they proceeded with their enemies, for they were the hereditary enemies of the Portuguese." The French trader explained to the Indians that Hans was a German and that he wanted to take him away. The Indians replied that they could not allow this, that Hans could be fetched only by his own father or brother who would have to appear with a ship laden with hatchets, mirrors and combs. The Frenchman then continued on his way.

While Hans awaited his end he was taken on an excursion by the Indians to a village called Tickquarippe where they were to feast on another prisoner. Hans advised him to take courage as the Indians would feast only on his body. His soul would then ascend to heaven. All then voyaged back to the home village. The Portuguese then sent a ship for Hans. On board they had goods for exchange, and when better informed of the situation, Hans' brother too. Actually, there was a Frenchman on board, a former companion of Hans. The Portuguese had been instructed to buy Hans, but he was not for sale.

Before his now long dreamed of liberation, Hans had more opportunity to observe the customs of the Indians. When one of their slaves from the Caribe tribe fell ill he was bled with the tooth of a rodent they called Backe (Pacca). Hans tried to do a more efficient job of bleeding by cutting into "the middle vein" but the tooth was too dull. The Indians predicted that the slave would die, then made certain of it by striking him on the head. Then contrary to Hans' advice, they ate him.

Soon a French ship put in seeking Brazilwood, pepper, monkeys and parrots. Hans attempted to negotiate his liberty but the Indians said that more goods would have to be brought in exchange for the prisoner. Hans bolted and swam for the ship, but the French pushed him away. They did not wish to annoy the Indians.

On August 13, 1554, Hans was taken on a war expedition which was part of the celebration of the Pirakien. At this time of year a fish called Bratti (Doynges in Portuguese) swam from salt to fresh water for spawning. The Indians left their village for the fish and for a battle with the Tuppinikin Indians. After the conflict they returned to their village with their captives, and feasting activities were begun. All the Indians danced and their prisoners were allowed to speak. Their speeches call to mind Montaigne's essay: "Yes, we went forth as it beseems valiant men, to capture and to eat you, our enemies. Now you have gained the upper hand, and have captured us, but we care not for this. Braves die in their enemy's country, and as our land is still large, the others will revenge as well upon you." The prisoners were then eaten.

At long last Hans' dismal tale changed. The French ship *Maria Bellette* which had rejected the Hessian would not have been his salvation anyhow. She had been lost en route to France. Soon another French ship put in at Rio de Janeiro, and the captain sent two men to the Tupinambá village. They were under orders to take Hans "to the ship, and to effect this they were to use every means." Hans did not attempt to divine why the French decided to rescue him from his plight, after all. Perhaps they pitied him. Perhaps they considered him a most useful agent for working with the Tupinambás. He quickly explained to his newest friends that his captors would have to be tricked, and that one of them would have to pose as his brother. Hans managed to get to the ship, and a plot was contrived. Ten of the French sailors became Hans' brothers and the captain gravely announced to the now impatient Indian chief, Abbati Bossange, that they all would hasten to France to bid farewell to their dying father. The chief wept but consented to the departure of Hans. The captains gave the Indians five ducats worth of knives and mirrors.

In October, 1554, the *Catherine de Vatta Ville* sailed out of Rio de Janeiro. The return voyage was comfortable. On February 20, 1555, the ship sailed into Honfleur harbor. Hans thanked Captain Guillaume de Moner for his kindness and prepared to leave. The captain suggested that Hans return with him to Brazil but Hans declined. He wanted to return to Hesse and a less eventful life.

In Hesse, Hans wrote about his adventures in Brazil, and the narrative was published in Marborg in 1557, then in Antwerp the following year. There were later German editions, several Dutch editions in the 17th century and in 1839 Hans' saga was included in Ternaux Compans' collection of voyages.

The Hessian's description of the Indians in Brazil was disorganized but written with simplicity and an abundance of detail. He described them as savage and with great variety in tribes and languages. Their land, he said, was "joyful." Their skins he described as "reddish-brown, on account of the sun which burns their bodies."

Hans reported that the Indians were clever hunters. They imitated the calls of their prey and shot them with bows and arrows. They also shot fish and could dive down more than thirty feet to bring the fish to the surface. They fished with nets too. Indians from the interior who fished in the ocean preserved the game by first baking the fish, then grinding it to a powder.

The Tupinambás devised their knives and axes from stone. With these they cut down trees for fuel for cooking. Their staple food was manioc, a tuber which each

family planted and harvested. From this six foot plant
they made a white flour, which was used for unleavened
cakes, byyw. The Tupinambás were among the few
Indians Hans saw who used salt. The majority spiced
their food with peppers. The Indians drank a fermented
manioc root beverage out of simple clay cups, fashioned,
painted and fired by the women. They sometimes drank
all night but did not dispute or harm one another.

Their villages were built close to wood and water.
When the wood in one location was used, they moved to
another and constructed a new village. Their huts were
about 14 feet wide and 150 feet long. In these open,
palm thatched huts the chief and others lived together.
Each family had its own fire. Surrounding the some seven
huts in the village was a protecting wall of split palm
trees with tiny holes for watching and shooting.

The chiefs were all-powerful but ruled leniently. The
young obeyed their elders.

Hans noticed that the Indians adorned themselves with
shells and feathers and the same green stone that Captain Gonneville mentioned. Their nails and hair were
long, and the style of their hair, a tonsure at the front
of the head with a cross on it, aroused Hans' curiosity.
When he inquired about it, he was informed that a man
called Meire (master) Humane had taught them that
and many other things. Scholars have speculated for
centuries on this curious prophet or the source of this
story. Perhaps Europeans or other foreigners had been
shipwrecked or had somehow reached Brazil before it
was officially discovered.[7]

The men named themselves after wild animals and ac-
quired another name every time they destroyed a foe.
The women were named after fruits, birds and fish. Most
men had one wife, but the chiefs often had more than

one. Wealth was measured in feathers, and the sign of wealth was a stone in the lower lip.

The Indians brought their god to them by cutting a hole in a pumpkin-like gourd, dropping stones in it, then instilling the object with power. This was called Tammarka and every man had his own. The Paygi, itinerant witchdoctors, transferred the power of speech and the ability to grant supplications to the Tammarkas. Hans carefully pointed out to his readers that the Tammarkas did not really speak, that, in fact, it was the soothsayer who spoke, but that the Indians did not perceive this.

For those who doubted the Hessian's remarkable story, he had this to say:

> Now, should there be any young man who is not satisfied with this writing and testimony, let him, so that he may not remain in doubt, with God's assistance, begin this voyage. I have herein given him information enough, let him follow the spoor; to him whom God helps, the world is not closed.

NOTES

1) Gaffarel, *Brésil français*, pp. 77-88.

Hans Stade, *Histoire d'un pays situé dans le nouveau monde, nommé Amérique* in series *Voyages et mémoires originaux pour servir à l'histoire de la découverte de l'Amerique*... edited by Henri Ternaux (Paris: Artus Bertrand, 1937), pp. 93, 110.

Guénin, *Ango*, p. 44. When La Pelerine sailed from Pernambuco in 1531, her cargo was:

5000 quintals of Brazilwood worth 8 ducats a quintal in France.

  300 quintals of cotton worth 5000 ducats a quintal.

  300 quintals of grain worth 3 ducats a quintal.

  600 parrots worth 6 ducats a parrot.

3000 leopard skins worth 3 ducats a skin.

      gold worth 3000 ducats.

      medicine worth 1000 ducats.

(one quintal equals 100 kilograms)

2) Gaffarel, *Brésil français,* p. 61. Details are from Jean de Léry, Andre Thevet, Hans Stade, and Portuguese who wrote about the Brazilians.

3) Montaigne, *Selected Essays,* ed. *Blanchard Bates* (New York: Modern Library, 1949), "Of Cannibals" pp. 74-89, quote 86-87. On eating, Montaigne reported that the Indians ate once a day. On wives, that each man had several, also that old wise men preached two things to the Indians "valor toward their enemies and love for their wives."

4) Andre Thevet, *Le Brésil et les Brésiliens,* intro. by André Julien (Paris: Presses Universitaires, 1953), p. vii.

5) Hans Stade, *The True History of his Captivity,* 1557. trans. and edited by Malcolm Letts, with intro. and notes (London: George Routledge & Son, 1928), p. 5.

   Gaffarel, *Brésil français,* p. 63.

   Julien, *Voyages de découverte,* pp. 91-92.

6) Stade, *Histoire d'un pays,* pp. 188, 126, 151-152, 176-177, 211, 217.

   The Captivity of Hans Stade of Hesse, in A.D. 1547-1555, Among the Wild Tribes of Eastern Brazil, tras. by Albert Tootal and annotated by Richard F. Burton, (Hakluyt Society, Ser. I, vol. 51). (New York, Burt Franklin), pp. 27-116.

7) *Tidings out of Brazil,* trans. by Mark Graubard, commentary and notes by John Parker (The University of Minnesota Press, James Ford Bell Collection Publication, 1957). This book contains the much discussed news letter *Copia der newen Zeytung ausz Presillg Landt* by an unknown author. It seems that he was not an eye-witness. Scholars do not agree on which voyage he was describing. Mr. Parker thinks that the evidence is in favor of the 1514 expedition which was commanded by João de Lisboa. The author described a prophet " . . . they cherish the memory of St. Thomas. They wished to show the Portuguese his footprints in the hinterland, and also to point out the cross standing in the interior. And when they speak of Saint Thomas they refer to him as the lesser god. There is, however, another god which is greater. It may well be believed that they do have memory of Saint Thomas for it is known that the body of this Saint is actually buried beyond Malacca on the coast of Siramatl (Coromandel) in the Gulf of Ceylon." p. 30.

   The explorer-mathematician R. Buckminster Fuller has developed a NA theory on early navigation. He suggests that the words navy, navigation, nautical sprang from the ancient word for the sea-NA. The serpent god of the sea was NAGA. Fuller thinks it not unlikely that man was drifting, then running before the wind, then tacking into it long before he was discussing it. Indeed, this magic, actually technological leap, may have been suppressed by the high priests-mariners. Fuller suggests that man went to sea possibly on the Japan current, and did not return home. Later, he developed a rudder and crude sails (perhaps first living trees). When man learned to sail close to the wind, there was no limit to his travel on the sea. He sailed to India, then to the Mediterranean. His technological know-how was impressive. He wonders if perhaps that is why Greece burst forth with quadratic equations. Man then crossed the Atlantic Ocean to North and South America. Perhaps the memory of one of these very early voyagers was preserved by the indians in Brazil and elsewhere in the New World.

"The New Yorker" Profile—"In the Outlaw Area" by Calvin Tomkins, pp. 90-92. (January 8, 1968).

8) *The Captivity of Hans Stade, Part the Second, A Veritable and Short Account of all the by me Experienced Manners and Customs of the Tuppin Imbas, Whose Prisoner I was.* pp. 119-169.

Tidings out of Brazil, pp. 28-33.

> "The people on that coast have no laws, nor have they a king. They do, however honor the elders among them and give obedience to them in the same manner as in lower Brazil. They are all one people although they speak another language . . .
>
> There are, namely, furs of lions and leopards which are numerous in the land, lynx and genet . . . There is also to be found much otter and beaver, an indication that the land has large flowing rivers . . .
>
> The country yields a wonderful abundance of fruits of good quality, and different from what we have in our lands . . . They also have beeswax, a gum similar to gloret, and many kinds of birds with rough feet . . .
>
> Their defensive weapons consist of hand bows as is the custom in lower Brazil. They have no iron mines. In exchange for an axe or hatchet or knife they give us whatever they have . . . They also have in that land a kind of spice which burns on the tongue as pepper, even stronger. It grows in a pod with many kernels growing within it . . .
>
> They (the Portuguese) have learned at the same location on the coast from the same people that further inland there is a mountain people having much gold.

VOYAGE
DU CAPITAINE PAULMIER DE GONNEVILLE
AU BRESIL
(1503-1505)

Annoté par Ch. A. Julien

RELATION AUTHENTIQUE[1]

LES GENS TENANTS L'ADMIRAUTE DE FRANCE

AU SIEGE GENERAL DE LA TABLE DE MARBRE
DU PALLAIS A ROUEN[2]
SCAVOIR FAISONS

QUE DES REGISTRES DU GREFFE DUDIT SIEGE,
ANNEE MIL CINQ CENS CINQ, A ESTE EXTRAIT ET
COLLATIONNE A LA MINUTTE ORIGINALE CE QUI
ENSUIT

PREMIERE PARTIE

DECLARATION DU VEGAGE
DU CAPITAINE GONNEVILLE
ET SES COMPAGNONS
ES INDES,

ET REMERCHES FAITES AUDIIT VEGAGE
BAILLEES VERS JUSTICE PAR EL CAPITAINE ET SES DITS
COMPAGNONS JOUSTE QU'ONT REQUIS LES GENS DU ROY
NOSTRE SIRE ET QU'ENJOINT LEUR A ETE

SECTION PREMIERE

Armement du navire

[*Origine et but de l'entreprise*]

Et[3] premièrement, disent que traficquant en Lissebonne[4], il Gonneville et honnorables hommes Jean l'Anglois et Pierre le Carpentier, veües les belles richesses d'épiceries et autres raretéz venant en icelle cité de par les navires portugalloises allant ès Indes orientales, empuis aucunes années découvertes, firent complot ensemblement d'y envoyer une navire, après bonne enqueste à aucuns qui avoient fait tel voyage, et pris à gros gages deux Portugallois qui en estoient revenus,[5] l'un nomme Bastiam Moura, l'autre Diègue Cohinto, pour en[6] la route ès Indie ayder de leur sçavoir.

[*Armateurs et navire*]

Et parce que ces trois devant dits n'avoient bastantes facultéz pour seuls mener à chef si haute enterprise, s'adjoignirent avecques honnorables hommes Etienne et Antoine dits Thiéry[7] frères, Andrieu de la Mare, Batiste Bourgeoz, Thomas Athinal et Jean Carrey, bourgeois de Honnefleur qui eux neuf, à fraiz et coustements communs, équipèrent un navire du pors[8] de six ving tonneaux, peu moins, dite[9] *l'Espoir,* qui n'avoit jamais servy qu'a faire un voyage en Hambourg, bon de corps et vesels, et des mieux équipéz de tous agrests, du hable[10] de Honnefleur; ne fut fait espargne par les bourgeois dudit navire pour le bien ammonitionner[11], et jouste l'inventaire de reveüe y avoit, sçavoir:

[*Armes et munitions de guerre*]

Pour ammonitions de guerre:

Deux pièces[12] de franche fonte de cuivre et léton;

Deux demies pièces en pareil de franche fonte;

Six que berches[13] et perrières[14] de fonte de fer de maintes grosseurs et charges.

Quarante que mousquets, harquebuses et autres tels bastons[15] à féu,

Seize cens pesants[16] de balles de différens calibres pour les artilleries, non en ce compris trois douzaines de balles à fiches et chaisnes,[17]

Plus en balles pour lesdits bastons à feu, que plomb en table et saulmon, quatre cens pesants;

En ferrailles et mintrailles[18] pour les dites artilleries, cinq cens pesants,[19]

Deux milliers de poudre à canon, dont y avoit la quinte part de grenée;

Trois cens cinquante de mesches à bastons à feu;

Les dites artilleries montées de leurs affusts, et garnies du nombre et quantité requise et ordinaire de refoulloirs[20] amanchés à tire-boure au bout, desgorgeoirs[21], escouvillons, plaques, laveret, coings de mire[22], pinces de mire et autres boutefeau,[23] gargouches tant de fer que de bois, peaux de parchemin et gros papier pour ce, trisses[24] garnies de poulies, dragues, et autres besognes requises;

Quarante que piques, demy-piques, pertuisanes et langue de boeuf;[25]

Item, plus, pour rechange;

Deux affusts;

Six roues d'affuts;

Douzaine et demye d'effet de fer aussy de rechange;

Six crocs à bassins pour tresses;[26]
Et quatre douzaines que goupilles et esquestreaux.

[*Matériel naval de rechange*]

Item en ammonition de naviage, pour rechange;
Deux ancres pardessus ceux d'ordinaire, pesant l'un cinq cens, l'autre trois cens;
Deux cables aussy de rechange, l'un des deux de six vingts brassés,[27] l'autre de cent;
Et deux cables de hauzière[28] aussy de rechange;
Et six cens aulnes tant de coutommine double que simple, toille escrue que royale[92] pour la rechange des vesles;
Huit cuirs pour les poupes et les vergues de beaupré;
Six hachettes aciérées pour couper les manœuvres,[30]
Une douzaine d'hachetts, que d'armes, que à main;
Et un timon et barre re rechange.

Et est tout ce vérifié vray par l'inventaire sus allégué, montre la grande perte que ledit capitaine et bourgeois ont faite par le pillement et sacage de leur navire, dont y a par eux plainte à Justice; en laquelle avoient obmis par inadvertance ou autrement, fair mention de la par quantité et espèce de ses ammonitions.

[*Victuailles*]

Plus fut ladite navire envitraillée de biscuit, grain, farine, pour viron[31] deux ans, eüe raison au nombre des gens de l'équipage;
Des poix, febves, lard, chèvres, et poissons saléz et séchéz, cidres et autres boissons, non compris la provision d'eau, pour un an et mieux;
Et si, outre fut garnie de force rafraischissement avant le départ;
Comme en pareil, le coffre du Chirurgien de ladite

navire atourné de maints médicaments de plus de requeste, et des engins et outils de son art.

[Marchandises de troque]

Pour marchandises fut chargée la navire:

De toilles diverses trois cens pièces;

De haches, bêches, serpes, coutres, fauches, du tout ensemble quatre milliers;

Deux mille de pignes, maintes sortes;

Cinquante douzaines de petits miroirs;

Six quintaux de rassades de voirre;[32]

Et huit de quinquailleries de Roüen;

Ving grosses de cousteaux et jambettes;[33]

Une balle d'épingles et égüilles;

Vingt pièces de droguet;[34]

Trente de futaine;

Quatre de draps teints écarlatte;

Huit autres de différentes façons;

Une de velours figuré;

Quelques autres dorées;

Et argent monoyé qu'ils avoient sceu être de receutte en Indie [plus] que l'or;

Et le tout, de mesme qu'ont acoustumé s'en charger les Portugallois, pour estre par delà et sur la route ces choses de meilleure traficque.

[Constitution de l'equipage et disposition de départ]

Disent qu'en la navire s'embarquèrent en tout soixante âmes; et du bon vouloir de trestous, et spécialement de cil des bourgeois de la navire, fut estably capitaine et chef principal iceluy de Gonneville, pour gouverner le végage à son mieux, avec l'advis de Andrieu de la Mare et Anthoine Thiéry,[35] des dits bourgeois de la navire, qui étoient du végage.

Et pour le mestier de la mer étoit pour pillotte Colin Vasseur, de Saint-Arnoux lèz de Touques,[36] bon vieux routier et maistre; et Nollet Epeudry de Grestaing, sous pilotte.

Et tous, tant principaux que compagnons, reçeurent avant partir leurs sacremens, tant pour la fortune d'un si loingtain végage que pour la doutance de ne les recevoir de longtemps pour ce qu'il n'y avoit de chapelain en la navire, et alloient hors chrétienneté.

Et ainsy s'en partirent du hable de Honnefleur le propre jour de Monseigneur saint Jean Baptiste,[37] l'an de grâce mil cinq cens trois.

SECTION DEUXIEME

Voyage d'aller

[De Honfleur au Cap Verd]

Disent outre, que partys, la mer afflorée de vent nord-est propice, en dix-huit jours ou viron parvinrent aux isles Canarres,[38] qui sont terres haultees, surtout la celle de Ténériffe, entre laquelle et la Gomarre passèrent sans s'y arrester, allant de là quérir Barbarie, costoyans ledit pays, qui est terre basse et razes campagnes.

De Barbarie furent quérir les isles de cap de Verd, pleines de monts et rocs, habitués demeurans Portugallois, qui la font leur principalle traficque de cabrètes, dont lesdites isles abondent.

Et outre passéz, parvinrent á la grande terre dudit cap de Verd,[39] pays à Maures, qui trocquèrent, avec ceux de la navire, du couchou, manière de ris, des poulles noires et autres victuailles, pour fer, rassades, et telles babiolles; dont ladite navire refraîchie, ensemble d'eaüe, et nétoyée de sapinettes: cy ayant pour ce demeuré dix jours.

[Du cap Verd à l'Equateur]

Item disent qu'eux remis en mer, la vigille Saint-Laurens[40] fut arresté de prende cours loing de la coste d'Affricque, pour éviter les dangers et pestilence de sa coste. Et avoient lors vent assez favorable, qui continua bien six sepmaines;[41] fors que parfois s'eslevoient des tourbillons en temps serain, qui tourmentoient fort, mais ne duroient guières. Et aussy étoient incommodéz de pluyes puantes, qui tachoient les habits; cheutes sur la chair, faisoient venir bibes,[42] et étoient fréquentes.

[Passage de la Ligne]

Item disent que la ligne de l'Equateur fust par eux outrepassée le douzième septembre; et virent, tant deçà que delà, à l'aller et revenir, des poissons volants par bandes comme feroient en France estourneaux, ayans ailes comme de sourisgaudes,[43] et aprochant en grosseur d'un harang blanc:[44] plus se voyent des dorées,[45] marsoincz et autres poissons, dont les matelots faisoient prise et chaudière.

Et lors commença en la navire le mal de mer,[46] dont bien les deux tiers de l'équipage fut affligé; et en moururent le sieur Coste d'Harfleur, qui de curiosité venoit au vegage, Pierre Estieuvre et Louys Le Carpentier d'Honnefleur, Cardot Hescamps artillier du Pont eau de mer, Marc Drugeon du Breuil, et Philippes Muris de Touques.

Et dès lors se commençoient à conduire par la Croisée de l'autre pôle.

[Rencontre de varechs flottants]

Item disent que huit jours après la Toussaint[47] virent

flottant en mer de longs et gros roseaux avecques leurs racines,[48] que les deux Portugallois disoient estre le signe du Cap de Bonne Espérance, qui leur fit grand joye; et parce qu'ils ne voyoient les oiseaux dits Manche-de-Velours,[49] estimoient la navire faire cours pas[50] bien au dessous dudit Cap, comme aussy de ce que sentoient un froid plus grand.

[Vent contraires]

Disent que lors commencèret[51] à avoir temps et vent contraire, si que par après de trois sepmaines n'avancèrent guières.[52] Et leur mourut Collin Vasseur, leur principal pilotte, d'apoplexie subite, qui fut la grande perte du végage.

Et fut ledit malheur suivy d'autre, sçavoir, de rudes tourmentes, si véhémentes, que contraints furent laisser aller, par aucuns jours, au gré de la mer, à l'abandon; et perdirent leur route; dont etoient for affligéz, pour le besoin qu'ils avoient d'eaüe, et se rafraichir en terre.

[Découverture d'une grande terre]

Disent que la tourmente fut suivie d'aucuns calmes, si qu'avançoient-ils peu. Mais Dieu les réconforta; car ils commencèrent à voir plusieurs oiseaux venans et retournans du costé du zud, ce qui leur fit penser que de là ils n'étoient éloignéz de terre: pour quoy, jaçoit qu'[53] aller là fust tourner le dos à l'Inde orientalle, nécessité cy fit tourner les vesles; et le cinq Janvier découvrirent une grande terre, qu'ils ne purent aborder que l'assoirant du lendemain, obstant un vent de terre contraire; et encrèrent à bon fond.[54]

Et dèz ledit jour aucuns de l'équipage furent en terre reconnoistre; et dez le matin suyvant fut envoyé la barge ranger la coste pour trouver port, et revint l'après-mydy;

et conduisit la navire dans une rivière qu'elle avoit trouvée, qui est quasiment comme la celle de Orne.

SECTION TROISIEME

Sejour ès nouvelles terres des Indes

[Etat du navire, et résolutions en conséquence]

Disent avoir séjourné audit pays jusques en Julliet suyvant, pour y avoir trouvé la navire si vermolue et gastée, qu'elle avoit grand besoin de rabout: à quoy fut employé non petit temps, pour le manque d'ouvriers experts ès[55] choses.

D'où les compagnons de la navire s'occasionnèrent de vouloir revenir en France, refusant naviger dudit lieu de l'Inde, disant ladite mer n'avoir esté encore navigée de Chrestiens, le temps estre perdu, le principal pilotte par pareil, en qui étoit la maistresse fiance du voyage; et qui plus fut, que ladite navire fut jugée ne pouvoir souffrir tel végage. Si que pour ces raisons et autres, que tretous signèrent pour la descharge du capitaine, fut aduisé le retour en Chrestienneté.

[Caractère et manière de vivre des [Indigènes]

Item disent que pendant leur demeurée en la dicte terre ils conversoient bonnement avec les gens d'icelle,[56] après qu'ils furent apprivoiséz avec les Chrestiens, au moyen de la chère et petits dons qu'on leur faisoit; estans lesdicts Indiens gens simples, ne demandant qu'à mener joyeuse vis sans grand travail; vivant de chasse et pesche, et de ce que leur terre donne de soy, et d'aucunes légumages et racines qu'ils plantent; allant my-nuds, les jeunes et communs spéciallement, portant manteaux,[57] qui de nattes déliées, qui de peau, qui de plumasseries, comme sont en ces pays ceux des Egiptiens et Boëmes, fors qu'ils sont plus courts, avec manière de tabliers ceints par sus les hanches, allans jusques aux genoux aux hommes, et aux femelles à my-jambe; car hommes et femmes sont accoutréz de même manière, fors que l'habillement de la femme est plus long.

Et portent les femelles colliers et brasselets d'os et coquilles; non l'homme qui porte au lieu arc et flesche ayant pour vireton un os proprement asseré, et un espieu de bois très dur brulé et asséré par en hault; qui est toute leur armure.

Et vont les femmes et filles teste nue, ayant leurs cheveux gentiment teurchéz de petits cordons d'herbes teintes de couleurs vives et luisantes. Pour les hommes, portent longs cheveux ballants, avec un tour de plumasses hautes, vive-teintes et bien atournées.

[*Fécondité du pays*]

Disent outre avoir entré dans ledit pays bien deux journées avant, et le long des costes davantage tant à dextre qu'à senestre; et avoir remerché ledit pays estre fertile, pourveu de force bestes, oiseaux, poissons, arbres, et autres choses singulières inconnues en Chrestienneté, dont feu monsieur Nicolle le Febvre d'Honfleur qui étoit volontaire au voyage, curieux, et personnage de sçavoir, avoit pourtrayé les façons; ce qui a esté perdu avec les journaux de végage lors du piratement de la navire; laquelle perte est à cause que[58] en sont maintes choses et bonnes remerches obmises.

[*Habitations*]

Item disent ledit pays être peuplé entre deux.

Et sont les habitations des Indiens par hameaux de

trente, quarante, cinquante, ou quatre vingts cabanes, faites en manières de halles de pieux fichéz joignant l'un l'autre, entrejoints d'herbes et feuilles, dont aussy lesdits habitans sont couverts; et y a pour cheminée un trou pour faire en aller la fumée. Les portes sont de bastons proprement liéz; et les ferment avec clefs de bois, quasiment comme on fait en Normandie, aux champs, les estables.

Et leurs lits sont de nattes douces pleines de feuilles[59] ou plumes, leurs couvertes de nattes, peaux, ou plumasseries; et leurs ustencilles de ménage, de bois, même leurs pots à bouillir, mais induis d'une manière d'argille bien un doigt d'espais, ce qui empesche que le feu ne les bruslast.

[*Gouvernement*]

Item disent avoir remerché ledit pays estre divisé par petits cantons, dont chacun a son Roy; et quoy que lesdits Roys ne soient guières mieux logéz et accoustréz que les autres, si est-ce qu'ils[60] sont moult révéréz de leurs sujets; et nul si hardy ose refuser leur obeïr, ayans iceux pouvoir de vie et mort sur leurs sujets: dont aucuns de la navire virent un exemple digne de mémoire, sçavoir, d'un jeune fils de dix-huit à vingt ans qui en certain chaud dépit avoit donné un soufflet à sa mère; ce qu'ayant sceu son seigneur, jaçoit que[61] sa mère n'en eust été à plainte, il l'envoya quérir, et le fit jetter en la rivière, une pierre au col, appelléz à cry[62] publique les jeunes fils du village et autres villages voisins; et si nul n'en put obtenir rémission, ny mesme la mère, qui à genoux vint requérir pardon pour l'enfant.

[*Le Roi et sa famille*]

Le dit Roy estoit le cil en la terre de qui demeura la navire; et avoit à nom Arosca. Son pays estoit de bien une journée, peuplé de viron une douzaine de villages, dont chacun avoit son capitaine particulier, qui tous obeïssoient audit Arosca.

Le dit Arosca estoit, comme il sembloit, âgé de soixante ans, lors veuf; et avoit six garçons depuis trente jusques à quinze ans; et venoit, luy et ses enfans, souvent à la navire. Homme de grave maintien, moyenne stature, grosset, et regard bontif; en paix auec les Roys voisins, mais luy et eux guerroyant des peuples qui sont dans les terres: contre lesquels il fut deux fois, pendant que la navire séjourna; menant de cinq à six cens hommes chacune fois. Et la dernière, à son retour fut démenée[63] grande joye par tout son peuple, pour avoir eu grande victoire; leurs dites guerres n'estans qu'excursions de peu de jours sur l'ennemy. Et eust bien eu envie qu'aucuns de la navire l'eust accompagné avec bastons à feu et artillerie, pour faire paour et desrouter[64] ses dits ennemys; mais on s'en excusa.

[*Distinctions extérieures.*]

Item disent qu'ils n'ont remerché aucunes merches particulières qui différentast ledit Roy et autres Roys dudit pays, dont il en vint jusques à cinq voir la navire, fors que lesdits Roys[65] portent les plumasses de leur teste d'une seule couleur; et volontiers leurs vassaux, du moins les principaux, portent à leur tour de plumasses quelques brins de plumes de la couleur de leur seigneur, qui estoit le verd pour celle dudit Arosca leur hoste.

[*Accueil fait aux Européens.*]

Item disent que quand les Chrestiens eussent esté anges descenduz du ciel, ils n'eussent pu estre mieux chéris par ces pauvres Indiens,[66] qui estoient tous esbahis de la grandeur de la navire, artillerie, mirouërs, et autres choses qu ils voyoient en la navire, et surtout de ce que par un mot de lettre qu'on envoyoit du bord aux gens de l'équipage qui estoient par les villages on leur faisoit sçavoir ce qu'on avoit volonté; ne se pouvant persuader comme le papier pouvoit parler. Aussy pour ce les Chrestiens estoient par eux redoubtéz, et pour l'amor d'aucunes petites libéralitéz qu'on leur faisoit de pignes, cousteaux, miroirs, rasades, et telles babiolles, si ayméz, que pour eux ils se fussent volontiers mis en quartiers, leur aportant foison de chair et poissons, fruits et vivres, et de ce qu'ils voyoient estre aggréable aux Chrestiens, comme peaux, plumasses, et racines à teindre; en contréchange de quoi[67] leur donnoit-on des quinquailleries et autres besongnes de petit prix: si que desdites danrées en fut bien amassé prèz de cent quintaux, qui en France auroient vallu bon prix.

[*Plantement d'une croix.*]

Item disent que voulant laisser merches audit pays qu'il y avoit là abordé des Chrestiens, fut faicte une grande croix de bois, haulte de trente-cinq pieds et mieux, bien peinturée; qui fut plantée sur un tertre à veüe de la mer, à belle et dévote cérémonie, tambour et trompette, sonant, à jour expréz choisy, sçavoir, le jour de la grande Pasques mil cinq cens quatre.[68] Et fut ladite croix portée par le capitaine et principaux de la navire pieds nuds; et aydoient ledit seigneur Arosca et ses enfants et autres greigneurs Indiens, qu'à ce on invita par honneur; et s'en montroient joyeux. Suivoit l'équipage en armes,[69] chantant la litanie, et un grand peuple d'Indiens de tout âge, à qui de ce longtemps devant on avoit fait feste, coys et moult ententifs[70] au mistère.

Ladite croix plantée, furent faites plusieurs décharges de scopeterie et artiellerie, festin et dons honnestes[71] audit seigneur Arosca et premiers Indiens; et pour le populaire, il n'y eut cil à qui on ne fist quelque largesse de quelques menues[72] babiolles de petit coust, mais d'eux prisées, le tout à ce que du fait il leur fust mémoire,[73] leur donnant à entente par signes et autrement, au moins mal que pouvoient, qu'ils eussent à conserver et honorer la-dite croix.

Et à icelle èstoit engravé, d'un costé, le nom de nostre Saint Père le Pape de Rome, du Roy nostre Sire, de Monseigneur l'Admiral de France;[74] du capitaine, bour-geois et compagnons d'empuis le grand jusques au plus petit. Es fist le carpentier de la navire cet œuvre, qui ly valut un présent de chasque compagnon. D'autre costé fut engravé un deuzain numbral latin de la façon de monsieur Nicole Le Febvre dessus nommé, qui par gen-tille manière déclaroit la datte de l'an du plantement de ladite croix, et qui plantée l'avoit; et y avoit:

HIC SACRA PAIMARIVS POSVIT GONIVILLA BINOTUS;
GREX SOCIVS PARITER, NEVSTRAQVE PROGENIES.[75]

[Dispositions pour le retour]

Disent outre qu'à la parfin la navire ayant esté radou-bée, gallifrestée, et munie au mieux qu'on peut pour le retour, fut arresté de s'en partir pour France.

Et parce que c'est coustume à ceux qui parviennent à nouvelles terres des Indes, d'en amener à Chrestienneté aucun Indiens, fut tant fait par beau semblant, que ledit seigneur Arosca vousist bien qu'un sien jeune fils qui d'ordinaire tenoit bon auec ceux de la navire, vint en Chrestienneté, parce qu'on promettoit aux[76] père et fils le ramener dans vingt lunes au plus tard; car ainsy[77] donnoient-ils entendre les mois. Et ce qui plus leur don-noit envie, on leur faisoit à croire qu'à cils qui viendroient par deçà on leur apprendroit l'artillerie; qu'ils souhai-

toient grandement, pour pouvoir maistriser leurs ennemys: comme estout[78] à faire miroüers, cousteaux, haches,
et tout ce qu'ils voyoient et admiroient aux Chrestiens;
qui estoit autant leur promettre que qui promettoit à un
Chrestien or, argent et pierreries, ou luy aprendre la pierre philosophale.

Lesquelles affaires creües fermement par ledit Arosca,
il estoit joyeux de ce qu'on vouloit amener son dit jeune
fils qui avoit à nom Essomericq; et luy donna pour com-
pagnie un Indien d'âge de trente cinq ou quarante ans
appellé Namoa. Et les vint luy et son peuple convoier à
la navire; les pourvoyant de forces vivres, et de maintes
belles plumasses et autres raretéz, pour en faire leurs
présens de sa part au Roy nostre Sire. Et ledit Seigneur
Arosca et les siens attendirent le départ de la navire, faisant jurer le capitaine de s'en revenir dans vingt lunes; et
lors dudit départ, tout ledit peuple faisoit un grand cry,
et donnoient à entente qu'ils conserveroient bien la croix;
faisant le signe d'icelle en croisant deux doigts.

SECTION QUATRIEME.

Voyage de retour

[*Gros temps et maladies.*]

Item disent qu'adonc partirent desdites Indes méri-
dionalles le tiers de Julliet cinq cens quatre, et depuis ne
virent terre jusques au lendemain Saint-Denys,[79] ayant
couru diverses fortunes, et bien tourmentéz de fièvre ma-
ligne, dont maints de la navire furent entachéz, et quatre
en trépassèrent, sçavoir: Jean Bicherel, du Pont-l'Eves-
que, chirurgien de la navire; Jean Renoult, soldat, d'Honfleur, Stenoz Vennier, de Gonneville sur Honfleur, valet

du capitaine; et l'indien Namoa.

Et fut mis en doubte de le baptiser, pour éviter la per-
dition de l'âme; mais ledit monsieur Nicole disoit que ce
seroit prophaner baptesme en vain, pour ce que ledit
Namoa ne sçavoit la croyance de nostre mère Sainte
Eglise comme doivent sçavoir ceux qui reçoivent[80] baptesme ayant âge de raison; et en fut creu ledit monsieur
Nicole comme le plus clerc de la[81] navire. Et pourtant
d'empuis en eut scrupule; si que l'autre jeune indien Essomericq estant malade sa fois, et en péril, fut, de son
advis, baptisé; et luy administra son sacrement ledit monsieur Nicole, et furent les parrains ledit de Gonneville
capitaine, et Antoine Thiéry,[82] et au lieu de marreine
fut pris Andrieu de la Mare pour tiers parrain; et fut
nommé Binot, du nom de baptesme d'iceluy capitaine:
ce fut le quatorzième septembre que ce fut fait. Et sem-
ble que ledit baptesme servit de médecine à l'âme et au
corps, parceque d'empuis ledit Indien fut mieux, se gué-
rit, et est maintenant en France.

[*Escale à une autre terre.*]

Disent là lesdites maladies estre prouenues pour s'estre
les eaüer de la navire gastées et ampuanties, et aussy
pour l'air de mer, comme peurent remercher, en ce que
l'air de terre et viandes et eaües fresches guérirent tous
les malades. Pour quoy, sçavants en la cause de leur mal,
souhaitaoient tretous terre.

Or passéz le Tropique Capricorne, hauteur prise,
trouvoient estre plus éloignéz de l'Affrique que du pays
des Indes occidentalles où d' empuis aucunes années en
çà les Dieppois et les Maloüinois et autres Normands et
Bretons vont quérir du bois à teindre en rouge, cotons,
guenons et perroquets et autres denrées:[83] si que le vent
d'Est, qu'ils ont remerché régner coustumièrement entre

ledit Tropicque et cil du Cancre, les y poussant, fut d'una-
nimité délibéré d'aller quérir cetuy pays, affin estout
de se charger des susdites marchandises, pour rescaper
les frays et voyage.

Et y parvinrent le lendemain Saint Denys comme et
dit cy-dessus.

[*Portrait des habitants.*]

Item disent que là ils trouvèrent des Indiens rustres,
nuds comme venants du ventre de la mère, hommes et
femmes; bien peu y en ayant couvrant leur nature; se
peinturant le corps, signamment de noir; lèvres troüées,
les trous garnys de pierres verdes proprement polies et
agencées; incisés en maints endroits de la peau, par ba-
lafres, pour paroistre plus beaux fils, ébarbéz, my-tondus.
Au reste, cruels mangeurs d'hommes; grands chasseurs,
pescheurs et nageurs; dorment pendus en lits faits comme
un rets, s'arment de grands arcs[84] et massues de bois, et
n'ont entre eux ne Roy ny Maistres: au moins n'en ont-
ils rien remerché.[85]

Au parsus habitent un beau pays, de bon air, terre
fertile en fruits, oiseaux et animaux; et la mer poisson-
neuse: les espèces dissemblades de celles d'Europe. Et
font leur pain et breuvage de certaines racines.

[*Malencontre chez ces Cannibales.*]

Disent outre qu'aux lieux dudit pays qu'ils abordèrent
y avoit eu jà des Chrestiens, comme estoit apparent par
les denrées de Chrestienneté que lesdits Indiens avoient:
aussy n'estoient-ils estonnéz de voir la navire; et pour
tant surtout craignoient-ils l'artillerie et harquebuses.

Et ayant bravement abordé terre, comme aucuns des
compagnons puisoient de l'eaüe, et autres estoient en
terre sans armes ne rien craignans, furent traitreusement

assaillis par iceux meschans Indiens, qui tuèrent un page
de la nauire nommé Henry Jesanne, prirent et emmenè-
rent dans les bois Jacques L'Homme dit La Fortune, soldat, et Colas Mancel, marinier, tous d'Honfleur; et furent
ces deux pauvres gens perdus, sans leur pouvoir donner
réconfort.

Plys y avoit encore enterre quatre hommes, qui gagnè-
rent la barge et se sauvèrent, tous navréz fors[86] un; et si,
un des dits mourut ore prime[87] qu'il fust monté en la
navire: iceluy estoit ledit monsieur Nicolle Le Febvre
sus-mentionné, qui, par curiosité dont il estoit plein, s'estoit descendu à terre: et, fut de tretous regretté, comme
méritant meilleure avanture; car il estoit prude, affable,
et de sçavoir.

[*Nouvelle relâche à cent lieues plus loin.*]

Item disent que ce piteux cas leur fit quitter le lieu de
ce malencontre, et amonter la coste bien cent lieues plus
amont; où ils trouvèrent des Indiens pareils en façon:[88]
mais de ceux-cyne reçeurent aucun tort; et quand ils en
eussent machiné, ils n'en fussent venus à chief, parceque
le cas advenu faisoit qu'on ne s'y fioit.

Et là, pendant que la navire y demeura elle fut chargée
de vivres et des marchandises dudit pays prédéclarées, en
la quantité plus à plein et en détail contenue en la plainte
et douléance baillée à Justice contre cils qui ont pillé la
navire: y recours. Et eussent lesdites marchandises vallu
deffrayer le végage et outre bon proffit, si la navire fust
venue à bon port.

[*Départ définitif.*]

Item disent qu'ils partirent dudit pays entre la Saint
Thomas et Noël cinq cens quatre,[89] ayant attrapé deux
Indiens; qu'ils cuidoient amener en France; mais dèz la

première nuit ils se coulèrent en mer, estant lors la navire à plus de troys lieües de coste: mais ces gallands
sont si bons nageurs que tels trajet ne les effrite.

[*Du Brésil aux Açores.*]

Item disent qu'eux demeuréz n'ont veu rien digne de
remerche par sus ce qu'ils virent en allant, fors que sept
à huit jours après le débouquement[90] virent un islet inha-
bité,[91] couvert de bois verdoyans, d'om sortoient des mi-
lliasses d'oiseaux, si tant[92] qu'aucuns se vinrent à jucher
sur les mats et cordages de la navire; et s'y laissoient
prende. Et paraissoient lesdits oiseaux gros en plume,
ainsçoit que iceux pluméz soient de menue corpulence.

Et dans cinq sepmaines, après maints louviages, d'un
vent du zur-ouest outrepassèrent la Ligne, et revirent
l'estoille du Nord.

Puis eurent vents variables, et aucunes tourmentes. Et
se rencontrèrent en une mer herbüe[93] jonchée de grandes
herbes, grenues de graine rondelette comme vesche ou
viron, s'entretenant par longs filaments; et si, la mer est
là si profonde, que, la sonde jettée, n'y fut trouvé fond.

Et enfin, croyant n'estre qu'à la hauteur des isles Canarres, advisèrent les Essors, et ancrèrent à la Fayal[94] le
neuf mars derrain; et là eurent des vivres et autres choses
dont avoient besoin. Lesdits Essors sont habituéz de Portugallois.

[*Attaque de pirates.*]

Et eux en mer, furent contrains par tempeste relacher
en Irlande pour radouber aucunes voyes d'eaüe en la
navire.

Et remés à vesles, navigèrent heureusement[95] jusques
au septième de May derrain, qu'à l'abord des isles de
Jersay et Grenesey, malheur volut qu'ils fissent rencontre

d'un fourban anglois, dit Edouard Blunth, de Pleimouth:
contre lequel fut advisé, de commun sens, de se deffen-
dre; ce qui fut fait, jusques à ce que de derrière lesdites
isles vint à paroistre autre fourban épineux, françois de
nation, sçavoir, le capitaine Mouris Fortin, breton, déjà
condamné pour pirateries. Et lors, pour n'estre la partie
esgalle, fallut s'aller eschouer à la coste, où les hommes
furent en partie sauvéz, et la navire froissée et perdue
avec tout ce qui estoit ens, fors ce que lesdits coursaires
eurent temps de piller avant que ladite navire fust ache-
vée de couler à fond.

Et y eut d'hommes pérys que tuéz, douze personnes,
et quatre depuis qui moururent en l'isle de leurs playes,
le tout ainsy que le contient plus à menu la plainte et
douléance qu'en ont baillée à Justice ledit capitaine de
Gonneville et ses compagnons; y recours.

Et les noms des deffuncts son: Nollet Espeudry, pilotte, tué d'un coup d'artillerie; Jean Davy, et Perrot fils
du dit Jean; Robert Vallasse; Guillaume Du Bois; Guillaume Marie; Anthoine Pain; Cardin Vastine; Jacques
Sueur; le frère dudit Jacques, nommé Henry; Robert Ma-
hieu; Claude Verrier; Andrieu de Rubigny; le bastard[96]
de Colué; Jean Le Boucher; et Marc Des Champs: tretous de Honfleur et Touques,[97] ou environs.

Et en l'isle aprirent les noms desdits coursaires, et les
maux et pirateries qu'ils sont[98] coustumiers exercer à l'environ et ailleurs.

[Rentrée à Honfleur.]

Item disent que de l'isle, après que cils qui estoient
navréz furent mieux, passèrent au port de la Hogue,[99]
où ils laissèrent trois malades, sçavoir, Pierre Toustain,
Pierre de la Mare, et le sieur de Sainct-Clerimonies.

Et le reste vint par terre gaigner Honfleur, où ils arri-

vèrent le vingtième May derrain passé, au nombre de
vingt-huict,[100] cynommez, sçauoir: il de Gonneville, cap-
pitaine; lesdits Thiery et De la Mare, bourgeois; les deux
Portugallois; les sieurs Potier, Du Mont, De la Rivière,
Du Ham, et De Bois-Le-Fort, tous jeunes avanturiers de
Honfleur; Jean Cousin l'aisné, autre dit le Jeune, Claude
Mignon, Thomas Bourgeoz, Alexis L'Amy, Collas Val-
lée, Guillaume Le Duc, Thomas Varin, Jean Poullain,
Gilles Du Four, Robert Heuzé, Liénard Cudorge, Henry
Richard, Jacques Richard, et Jean Bosque, tous du mes-
tier de la mer; Lienard Cavalier, et Thomas Bloche,
pages.

Plus l'indien Essomericq, autrement dit Binot, qui
audit Honfleur et par tous les lieux de la passée, estoit
bien regardé, pour n'avoir jamais eu en France personnage de si loingtain pays: estant les gens de la ville aises
de voir leurs compatriotes revenus de tel et si grand
voyage, et marrys des cas malencontreux advenuez quasiment au seüil de l'hostel.

[*Motifs de cette déclaration.*]

Item disent qu'aux fins d'en avoir, Dieu aydant, quelque jour la réparation, ils ont, cux et les bourgeois ayant
part à la navire, baillé leurs douléances et articles à
Justice.

Et que les gens du Roy nostre Sire qui les ont reçeus,[101]
auroient requis que pour la rareté dudit voyage, et jouste
les ordonnances de la marine portantes que à la Justice
seront bailléz les journaux et déclarations de tous voyages
de long [cours], que ledit capitaine et compagnons fissent ainsy: pour quoy, obéissant à Justice, il capitaine de
Gonneville, et lesdits Andrieu de La Mare et Anthoyne
Thiéry,[102] qui ont esté chiefs présents à tout le voyage,
nc pouvant, à leur regret, bailler aucuns[103] de leurs jour-

naux, pour avoir esté perdus avecques la navire, ont fait la présente déclaration; le tout affirmant vray à Justice, et comme tel baillé, ce jour d'huy dix-neufième Juin mil cinq cens et cinq; et l'ont signé.

Ce que dessus extraict des Registres susmentionnéz, et collationné à sa minutte, saine et entière, deüement signée: lesdits registres représentéz, par le garde d'iceux obéissant aux lettres-royaux en forme de compulsoire[104] obtenus par damoiselle Marie Collet et joints, dont la teneur ensuit.

DEUXIEME PARTIE

LETTRES ROYAUX EN FORME DE COMPULSOIRE
PORTANT MANDEMENT
POUR LA DELIVRANCE D'EXTRAIT OU VIDIMUS
DE LA DECLARATION DU VOYAGE
DU CAPITAINE DE GONNEVILLE.

Loüis, par la Grâce de Dieu Roy de France et de Navarre.

A nos amés et féaux les Gens tenant nostre siège général de l'Admiraulté de France, à la Table de Marbre de Nostre Palais à Roüen, Salut.

Remonstré nous a esté de la part de Damoiselle Marie Colleth des Boves, veufve de feu Sieur Paulmier, sieur de Courthoyne et du Pommeret, tutrice de leurs enfans mineurs; comme aussi de la part des enfans majeurs dudit feu sieur du Pommeret; et[105] de Damoiselle Simonne Paulmier, vefve du sieur Le Doux, sieur de la Rozière, joints à ladite de Colleth.[106]

Qu'ayant esté depuis quelque temps en çà par nous ordonné que les estrangers et descendans d'iceux seroient

tant priéz[107] subveni raux necessitéz de nostre Estat; les
Préposéz[108] au recouvrement desdits deniers auroient
voulu comprendre en leurs poursuittes icelle vefve Collet,
bien qu'elle soit d'une famille sy constamment originaire
ddes pays de nostre obéissance, qu'elle peut justifier comme il y a trois cens ans ou viron qu'un de ses ayeuls servoit
avec employ de capitaine sous le connestable Bertrand
du Guesclin;[109] que la terre et [seigneurie][110] de Boves en
nostre comté d'Auge, entrée par un mariage en la famille de Collet, est possédée par ceux de ladite famille
par desja huit degréz de génération, et qu'en l'annee
mil quatre cens soixante et six, en la recherche faicte des
nobles de nostre province de Normandie par Monsieur
Remond de Montsault commissaire à ce député, Guillaume Collet sieur des Boves, quart ayeul de l'exposante
auroit esté trouvé issu de famille joüissante des lors, en
ladite vicomté, du privilège de noblesse depuis et par
temps immémorial, ce qui faict assez marquer qu'on ne
peut accuser sadite famille d'aubeinage, ni laditte Collet
pareillement, puis qu'estant née dans nos royaumes, de
gentilhommes originaires françois, et toujours vescu en
France, elle n'a pu contracter aucune qualité estrangère;
Qu'aussy les traictans desdites taxes disent particuliè-
rement la comprendre comme vefve et tutrice des soub-
sagez dudit feu sieur de Pommeret et d'elle; ce qui auroit
obligé les autres leurs enfants majeurs, ensemble ladite
Damoiselle vefve dudit sieur de la Rozière, soeur dudit
feu sieur du Pommeret, de se joindre à icelle exposante
pour soustenir: qu'encor qu'ils ne puussent méconnoistre
que Bynot Paulmier autheur de leur famille en nostre
royaume, ne fust d'origine estranger, et n'aye esté natu-
ralisé, néantmoins ils doivent demeurer exempts des re-
cherches, pour avoir esté ledit Binot amené des Indes par
un navire françois, comme ambassadeur et sous promesse

de la ramener au pays de sa naissance dans certain temps,
à laquelle promesse n'auroit esté satisfait, et d'ailleurs impossible audit Binot retourner à un pays si éloigné; et
qu'ainsy il ne serait juste que celluy qui est venu et demeuré en France en cette manière, et sa postérité, fussent
traictés de même sorte que les autres estrangers qui s'y
sont venus volontairement habituer, n'estant raisonnable
que lesdits descendans d'icelluy Binot, soient maintenant
inquiétéz parce qu'autrefois on ne leur a tenu les promesses faictes;

Et d'autant que la principalle pièce justificative de
cette leur deffense est une déclaration d'un voyage faict
auxdictes Indes par autre Binot Paulmier dit vulgaire-
ment le capitaine de Gonneville, baillée en Juin mil cinq
cens cinq par devers les officiers de nostre Almirauté
à Roüen, ainsy que anciennement par louable justifica-
tion estoit observé par tous capitaines et gens de mer
revenans de voyages de long cours; [111] et que d'autre costé
lesdits exposants n'ont l'original de cette pièce, qu'ils
prétendent décisive du procèz, mais seulement une coppie, que les dits traictans soustiennent ne pouvoir faire
foy, demandant la représentation de l'original; chose impossible aux exposants, parce que, par la disposition de
la Coustume de nostre dite prouvince de Normandie, les
ainsnéz doivent estre saisis de tous et chacuns les tiltres
concernant l'estat des familles, et les puisnéz en avoir
seulement coppies; suivant quoy feu amé et féal conseiller monsieur Jean Baptiste Paulmier, vivant premier
président des Thrésoriers de France en Provence, aisné de
ladite famille, auroit esté autrefois saisy dudit original,
ainsy qu'il seroit mentionné au pied et dans la collation
de ladite coppie; lequel feu Président s'estant habitué
audit pays de Provence, éloigné de plus de deux cens
lieües de domicile des exposants, et d'ailleurs n'ayant

laissé des masles qui eussent intérest à la conservation de tels tiltres, mais seulement une fille mariée audit pays au sieur de Fourbin marquis de la Barben;[112] il est évident que c'est chose comme impossible, du moins très-difficile à ladite vefve et joints de recouvrer ledit original, veu d'abondant la longueur du laps de temps, la grande distance des lieux, et autres circonstances cy-dessus touchées;

C'est pourquoy ils désireroient en avoir un Extrait ou Vidimus authentique, tiré des Registres de vostre greffe; mais ils doubtent que n'en fissiez difficulté, pour estre la déclaration dudit voyage contenue, ainsy qu'ils ont appris, aux registres du secret dudit Siège, si sur ce il ne leur estoit par Nous pourveu de lettres de compulsoire, que accordés leur avons de nostre grâce spéciale.[113]

A ces causes,

Nous vous mandons que sy dans lesdits Registres, même en ceux du secret et extraordinaire, est ladite Déclaration du voyage dudit cappitaine de Gonneville, ayez à en deslivrer ou faire deslivrer aux Exposants, Extraicts ou Vidimus[114] dont requis seréz. Et en cas de reffus ou délay, mandons au premier nostre[115] huissier ou sergent sur ce requis, faire tous explois et commandements qu'il appartiendra pour l'exécution[116] de ces présentes, résultantes de cas civil.

Car tel est nostre plaisir.

Donné à Roüen le dix-septième jour d'Aoust, l'an de grace mil six cens cinquante-huiet, et de nostre règne le seizième.

Signé: Par le conseil, COQUART, avec paraphe; et scellé d'un sceau de cire jaulne sur simple queüe.

Dont du tout avons fait expédier le présent, auquel nous avons fait apposer le scel, et icelluy faict délivrer pour [valoir l'original] et pour servir ce qu'il appartiendra à[117] ladite damoiselle Collet vefve dudit feu sieur de Pommeret tutrice desdits anfans, ladite vefve dudit de la Rozière, et autres joints et[118] consorts.

Donné audit Siège général, le trentième jour d'Aoust mil six cens cinquante-huit.

Martel.

Carmille.

NOTES

1) L'Indien Essomericq, emmené du Brésil en Normandie, se fixa à Honfleur après le naufrage de *l'Espoir* et épousa une des proches parentes de son parrain le capitaine Paulmier de Gonneville, dont il hérita le nom et une partie des biens. Ses descendants se virent réclamer, en 1658, des taxes d'aubaine en tant qu'issus d'étranger. Ils protestèrent que leur aïeul n'était pas venu demeurer en France de son plein gré, mais qu'il avait eu l'intention de regagner son pays après un court séjour, ce qu'il ne put faire, en dépit des promesses qu'il avait reçues, pour des raisons de force majeure. En conséquence, ils dénièrent aux traitants le droit de leur réclamer des taxes et présentèrent, à l'appui de leurs affirmations, le rapport établi par Gonneville à son retour, dont le tribunal fit vérifier l'authenticité par le grossoyement d'une expédition régulière. Les traitants furent déboutés de leur demande.

2) L'amirauté représentait, sous l'ancien régime, le corps à la fois administratif et judiciare à qu incombait de veiller à l'exécution des ordonnances et au respect des droits de l'amiral. En tant que juridiction d'exception, non souveraine, exércée par l'amiral. elle fonctionnait dans les principaux ports et connaissait de toutes les causes concernant la police et le commerce maritimes, tant au civil qu'au criminel. Comme tribunal, elle constituait, avec la connétablie et les eaux et forêts, les trois juridictions de la Table de marbre. Les juridictions tiraient leur nom de la table placée dans la grande salle du Palais, autour de laquelle elles se réunissaient. Il en existait d'analogues dans les parlements de province.

3) *Ms*: cet.

4) *Ms*: lislebonne.

5) Le gouvernement portugais conservait jalousement le secret des

routes maritimes à la fin du XV siècle, en répadant de faux renseignements, en réservant le monopole de la confection des cartes marines à des families súres et en contraignant les marins au silence. En dépit des sanctions qui frappaient l'aide donnée à des étrangers à l'égal d'un acte de trahison, des pilotes de Lisbonne, attiés par l'appàt du gain, prétaient leur concours aux interlopes qui voulaient trafiquer aux Indes.

6) *Ms*: et.

7) *Ms*: Thury. D'après l'abbé Paulmier, if faut lire Thierry.

8) *Ms*: pois. Le port du navire est ce qu'il peut porter de charge.

9) *Ms*: dit.

10) Corruption du mot *havle,* provenant du bas latin *haula* et s'appliquant à tous les ports de mer.

11) Approvisionner.

12) *Ms*: piecces.

13) D'après Cleirac (E,), *Termes de marine,* 1634, "berches sont petites pièces de fonte verte".

14) Corruption de *pierrier,* sorte de mortier qui permettait de lancer des pierres et des grenades.

15) Au Moyen-Age, toutes les armes droites, lances, massues, épées, étaient désignées sous le nom generique de *baston.* Après l'utilisation de la poudre, on distinua les armes portatives à feu par la dénomination de *bastons à feu.*

16) Pésants de livres, c'est-à-dire livres.

17) Balles traversées d'une barre de fer apointée des deux côtés dont on se servait pour offenser le navire ennemi.

18) D'après un manuscrit du XVI siècle: "Mitraille est toute sorte de vieux clous et autre ferraille, dont on se sert pour charger les Pierriers."

19) *Ms*: pensants.

20) Cylindre de bois dur, emmanché d'une longue hampe, qui servait à enfoncer el presser dans le fond du canon la charge qui devait chasser le projectile de la pièce.

21) *Ms*: desgorgeons. Appareils servant à enlever les matières qui encombraient la lumière du canon.

22) Pièces de bois placées sur la culasse d'un canon pour le pointage.

23) Bâtons garnis d'une méche pour mettre le feu au canon.

24) *Ms*: trises. Les trisses ou drosses sont les palans de côté et les palans de recul d'un canon.

25) Dagues.

26) Sorte de cordage fait de trois à neuf, et même plus, fils de caret ou de bitord dont on confectionne des tresses à la main.

27) La brassée ou brasse est une mesure de longueur pour les cordages, variable suivant les marines.

28) Les câbles de haussière ou d'aussière étaint des cordages commis avec trois torons ou masses de fil de caret tordus et dont la circonférence ètait moindre que celle des câbles de remorque.

29) *Ms*: noyale.

30) Cordages servant à soutenir les màts.

31) *Ms*: veron = environ.

32) *Ms*: rusades. Les rassades étaient des perles de verre ou d'émail, généralement d'origine vénitienne, fort appreciees des indigenes et qui jouaient un très grand rôle dans le troc.

33) Couteau pliant se mettant en poche.

34) *Ms*: drogues. Tissu, parfois tout de laine, plus souvent à chaine et trame dissemblables, généralement de bas prix et, à cause de cela, fort utilisé pour le troc.

35) *Ms*: Thury.

36) *Ms*: le dit Tougues.

37) Le 24 juin.

38) Les Canaries en travers desquelles *l'Espoir* arrive le 12 juillet.

39) Le 30 juillet.

40) Le mercredi 9 aoùt.

41) Approximativement jusqu'au 20 septembre, après avoir franchi l'équateur le mardi 12 septembre.

42) Ces bubes sont des boutons ou ampoules qui se développent sur la peau.

43) Les dactyloptéres de l'Atlantique ont des pectorales très vastes qui leur permettent de s'élever jusqu'à un mètre au-dessus de l'eau, comme avec des ailes.

44) Des exocets.

45) Nom vulgaire du zée forgeron (*Zeus faber*), dit aussi truie ou poisson saint-Pierre, de la famille des Scombridés.

46) Le scorbut.

47) Le jeudi 9 novembre.

48) Il ne peut s'agir de varechs flottans, comme l'écrit Avezac, p. 64, parce que les varechs sont des algues qui n'ont point de racine. Par contre, il existe une espèce de la famille des Joncées, le *Prionium serratum,* qui ressemble aux fuccas et abonde dans les riviéres de l'Afrique australe dont il obstrue parfois

le cours. Il n'est pas impossible que les eaux douces les arrachent et emportent en haute-mer.

49) Le fou dactylatre (*Sula dactylatra*) ou manche de velours, au plumage blanc avec lequel contrastent les remiges d'un noir velouté, est très commun dans l'Atlantique sud, notamment dans l'ile de l'Ascension.

50) *Ms*: par.

51) *Ms*: commençoient.

52) C'est-à-dire vers le 30 novembre.

53) Bien que.

54) L'*Espoir* dut aborder, le 6 janvier 1504, sur la côte du Brésil, au sud du tropique, entre Cananea et les lacs du sud, vers le 26 lat. S., aux pieds de la Serrado-Mar, où s'épanouit la forêt tropicale. Avezac a émis l'hypothèse que la rivière pourrait être l'ancien Rio Alagado, embouchure septentrionale du Rio San Francisco do Sul.

55) *Ms*: et.

56) Il s'agit vraisemblablement de la tribu guarani des Carijo (*Cario, Chandul*). Les Guarani occupaient, au début du XVI siècle, tout le litoral de l'Atlantique entre la Barra de Cananea et le Rio Grande do Sul.

57) D'autres voyageurs (Staden, Soarez de Souza, Lozana) ont signalé le port du manteau de peau par les tribus guarani.

58) *Ms*: qui. L'abbé Paulmier a lu qu'icy.

59) Généralement de palmiers.

60) *Ms*: qui.

61) Quoique.

62) *Ms*: appellée accry.

63) *Ms*: demeurée.

64) *Ms*: desroute.

65) *Ms*: et.

66) Les autres voyageurs confirment que les Carijo constituaient, comme l'écrivait le chroniqueur brésilien Simâo de Vasconcelos, "la meilleure nation du monde".

67) *Ms*: qui.

68) Le 7 avril.

69) *Ms*: et.

70) *Ms*: attentifs.

71) *Ms*: donnée honneste.

72) *Ms*: mesme.

73) *Ms*: memoré.

74) Le pape Alexandre VI, le roi de France Louis XII èt l'amiral français Mallet de Graville.

75) "Ici Paulmier de Gonneville éleva ce monument sacré, en associant intimement les peuplades et la lignée normande." Le chronogramme en forme de distique latin contient un M (1000) trols C (300), trois L (150), un X (10), sept V (35) et neuf I (9), ce qui donne le nombre 1504, désignant to millésime.

76) *Ms*: au.

77) *Ms*: aussy.

78) *Ms*: estoit.

79) Le 10 octobre.

80) *Ms*: recenoient.

81) *Ms*: du.

82) *Ms*: Tury.

83) C'est en se fondant sur ce texte que certains historiens attribuent aux Français la découverte du Brésil mais la chronologie de Gonneville est parfois fort peu précise et ne permet pas de contester la priorité des Portugais, au moins celle de Pedro Cabral, en 1500.

84) *Ms*: arcts.

85) Ce texte présente la première description, en français et par un Français, du sauvage nu, au corps noirci de suc de génipa ou balafré, portant des labrets de pierre verte, pratiquant le canniballisme et vivant dans l'anarchie. Si l'escale eut lieu vers Porto-Seguro, il ne peut s'agir que de Tupiniquin qui occupaient la côte depuis Cananea au nord, jusqu'au Rio S. Matheus au sud.

86) *Ms*: fort.

87) *Ms*: ore prime.

88) Sans doute des Tupinamba de la région de Bahia.

89) Entre le 21 et le 25 décembre. C'est là un exemple des imprécisions chronologiques des hommes du XVI siècle, qui se contentaient du temps mouvant comme l'a montré Febvre, *Le Probléme de l'incroyance au XVI siècle. La Religion de Rabelais,* 1942.

90) *Ms*: débougement.

91) D'après Avezac, Bahia est le seul point dont la disposition hydrographique puisse donner lieu à un débouquement, c'est-à-dire a un "passage de sortie." En pareil cas, l'île serait Fernam de Noronha, distante d'un millier de kilomètres, ce qui

correspond bien à une traversée d'une huitaine de jours et où pullulent les oiseaux, peut-être en l'occurrence les mouettes cendrées.

92) *Ms*: tost.

93) La mer des Sargasses dont les algues brunes couvrent une superficie de 4 millions de kilomètres carrés et qui a l'aspect d'un immense marécage et, par endroits, d'un pré vert-jaunâtre.

94) Après avoir reconnu les Açores, l'*Espoir* fait escale au Fayal, une des iles du groupe, le dimanche 9 mars.

95) *Ms*: heureux.

96) *Ms*: le Bastart.

97) *Ms*: Tonques.

98) *Ms*: ont.

99) *Ms*: la hoque.

100) Après deux ans de navigation, il ne survécut que vingt-sept hommes sur cinquante-huit.

101) *Ms*: reueu.

102) *Ms*: Thury.

103) *Ms*: autant.

104) Le compulsoire est la voie par laquelle un tiers est autorisé à prendre communication d'une pièce chez un dépositaire public et à s'en faire délivrer copie.

105) Le mot *et* manque dans le manuscrit.

106) Un des fils d'Essomericq, Binot Paulmier, sieur de Courthoyne ou Courtonne eut plusieurs enfants parmi lesquels une fille, Simonne Paulmier, mariée au sieur Le Doux, seigneur de La Rozière, et un fils putné, Olivier Paulmier, sieur de Courtonne et du Pommeret, marié à Marie Collet des Doves. C'est de ce dernier mariage que naquit Jean Paulmier de Courtonne, chanoine de la cathédrale de Saint-Pierre-de-Lisieux qui, en souvenir de son ancêtre, voulut établir une mission en pays sauvage.

107) *Ms*: prier.

108) *Ms*: proposer.

109) *Ms*: Guesclij.

110) *Ms*: le mot est demeuré en blanc dans le manuscrit.

111) *Ms*: coins.

112) La fille unique de Jean-Baptiste Paulmier et de Marquise d'Andrea époussa, le 4 mai 1625, Jacques de Forbin, seigneur de La Barbent.

113) *Ms*: vostre.

114) Attestation par les juges royaux qu'ils ont lu ou examiné un acte dont la teneur est manuscrite à la suite de cette déclaration.
115) *Ms*: vostre.
116) *Ms*: exemption.
117) *Ms*: et.
118) *Ms*: a.

BIBLIOGRAPHY

(Printed sources)

1.—AVEZAC, ARMAND D': *Campagne du navire l'Espoir, de Honfleur, 1503-1505. Relation authentique du voyage du capitaine de Gonneville es nouvelles terres des Indes, publiée intégralment pour la premiere fois avec une introduction et des éclaircissements par M. d'Avezac*. París: Challamel, 1869.

2.—BREAD, CHARLES ET PAUL: *Documents relatifs à la marine normande et a ses armemants aux XVIe et XVIIe siècles. Pour le Canada, l'Afrique, les Antilles, le Brésil et les Indes. Recueillis annotés, et publiés par Charles et Paul Bréard*. Rouen: Lestringant, 1889.

3.—*Byron's Journal of his Circumnavigation, 1764-66*. Edited by Robert Gallagher. Cambridge: University Press, for the Hakluyt Society, ser. 2, vol. 122, 1964.

4.—*Copy of a Lettèr to the King of Portugal sent to the King of Castile concerning the Voyage and Success of India*. Trans. by Sergio J. Pacifici. Minneapolis: University of Minnesota Press, 1955.

5.—CORREA, GASPAR: *The Three Voyages of Vasco da Gama and His Viceroyalty from the Lendas da India of Gaspar Correa accompanied by original documents.* Trans. and notes by Hon. Henry E. J. Stanley. New York: Fort Franklin, the Hakluyt Society, ser. 1, vol. 42.

6.—CORTES, HERNANDO: *The Despatches of Hernando Cortés, the Conqueror of Mexico, addressed to the Emperor Charles V*. With introduction and notes by G. Folsom. New York: Wiley and Putnam, 1843.

7.—DAVENPORT, FRANCIS GARDINER: *European Treaties bearing*

on the history of the United States and its dependencies. Vol. 1 to 1648. Washington: Carnegie Institution, 1917.

8.—*Diário da Viagem de Vasco da Gama.* Série Ultramarino, no. IV, Porto: Livraria Civilizacão, 1945.

9.—FREVILLE DE LORME, ERNEST: *Mémoire sur le commerce maritime de Rouen depuis les temps les plus reculés jusqu'à la fin de XVIe siècle, I.* París: Chez August Durant, 1857.

10.—GOSSELIN, EDOUARD HIPPOLITE: *Documents authentiques et inédits pour servir à l'histoire de la marine normande et du commerce Rouennais pendent les XVIe et XVIIe siècles.* Rouen: Imprimerie de Henry Boissel, 1876.

11.—GREENLEE, WILLIAM BROOKS: *The Voyage of Pedro Alvares Cabral to Brazil and India from contemporary documents and narratives.* London: Hakluyt Society, 1938.

12.—GUENIN, EUGENE: *Ango et ses pilots d'après documents inédits tirés des archives de France, de Portugal, et d'Espagne.* París: Imprimerie Nationale, 1901.

13.—JULIEN, CHARLES ANDRE: *Les Français en Amerique pendant la première moitié du XVIe siècle.* Colonies et Empires, deuxieme série, Les Classiques de la Colonisation, I. Paris: Presses Universitaries de France, 1946.
(Mainly narratives of voyages, this book includes the textual extract of the declaration of the voyage of *l'Espoir* and the Lettres Royaux.)

14.—LEY, CHARLES DAVID, ED.: *Portuguese Voyages 1498-1663.* London: J. M. Dent & Sons, 1947.

15.—MAJOR, R. H., ED.: *Early Voyages to Terre Australis now called Australia.* New York: Burt Franklin, Hakluyt Society, ser. 1, vol. 25.

16.—MARGRY, PIERRE: *Les Navigations françaises et la révolution maritime du XIVe au XVIe siècle d'après les documents inédits tirés de France, d'Angleterre, d'Espagne, et d'Italie.* París: Librarie Tross, 1864.

17.—*Os Sete Unicos Documentos de 1500 conservados em Lisboa, referentes a viagem de Pedro Alvares Cabral.* Lisboa: Agencia Geral das Colónias, 1940.

18.—PARKER, JOHN, ED.: *Tidings out of Brazil.* Minneapolis:

University of Minnesota Press, James Ford Bell Foundation, 1957.

19.—SKELTON, R. A.: *Explorers' Maps, Chapters in the Cartographic Record of Geographical Discovery*. London: Routledge and Kegan Paul, 1958.

20.—STADE, HANS: *Histoire d'un pays situé dans le nouveau monde, nommé Amérique, série voyages et mémoires originaux pour servir a l'histoire de la découverte de l'Amérique...* Ed. Henri Ternaux. París: Artus Bertrand, 1837.

21.—STADE, HANS: *The True History of his Captivity, 1557*, trans. ed. Malcolm Letts. London: George Routledge & Son, 1928.

22.—STADE, HANS: *The Captivity of Hans Stade of Hesse in A.D. 1547-1555, among the wild tribes of Eastern Brazil.* Trans. Albert Tootal, annot. by Richard Burton. New York: Burt Franklin, Hakluyt Society, ser. 1, vol. 51.

23.—WEINSTEIN, DONALD: *Ambassador from Venice, Pietro Pasqualigo in Lisbon, 1501.* Minneapolis: University of Minnesota Press, 1960.

OTHER SOURCES

1.—*Africa Pilot, vol. I, comprising Arquipélago Dos Açores, Arquipélago da Madeira, Arquipélago de Cabo Verde, and Islas Canaries, also the West Coast of Africa from Cabo Espartel to Calabar River.* London: Hydrographic Department, 1953.

2.—BARROS, JOAO DE: *Primeira Década da Asia.* Lisboa: Livrarias Aillanud e Bertrand, 1921.
(The author was five years old when Cabral sailed for India and reached Brazil en route.)

3.—BLAKE, JOHN WILLIAM: *European Beginnings in West Africa 1454-1578, a survey of the first century of white enterprise in West Africa with special emphasis upon the rivalry of the great powers.* London: Longmans, Green, 1937.

4.—CORTESAO, ARMANDO AND MOTA, AVELINO TEIXEIRA DA: *Portugaliae Monumenta Cartographica.* Lisboa: 1960.
(Five volumes of Portuguese cartography drawn up on the occasion of the 500th anniversary of the death of the Infante Henry.)

5.—DIFFIE, BAILEY W.: *Prelude to Empire, Portugal overseas before Henry the Navigator.* University of Nebraska, 1960.

6.—GAFFAREL, PAUL: *Histoire du Brésil Français au seizième siècle.* París: Maisonneuve, 1878.

7.—GALVAO, ANTONIO: *Tratado dos Descobrimentos Antigos e Modernos.* Porto: Livraria Civilizacão, 1963.

8.—JAL, AUGUSTE: *Glossaire Nautique, Repertoire Polyglotte de termes de marine anciens et modernes.* París: Firmin Didot Frères, 1848.

9.—JULIEN, CHARLES ANDRE: *Les Voyages de découverte, et les premiers établissements, XV, XVIe siècles Colonies et Empires,* 3 ser. *Histoire de l'expansion et de la colonisation françaises, I.* París: Presses Universitaires de France, 1949.

10.—LA RONCIERE, CHARLES DE: *Histoire de la Marine Française,* vol. III, *Les Guerres d'Italie Liberté des mers.* París: Librairie Plon, 1906.

11.—LAVISSE, ERNEST ED.: *Histoire de France, depuis les origines jusqu'à la revolution.* Vol. V, I, par Henri Lemonnier, 1492-1547. París: Hachette, 1911.

12.—MACLYSAGHT, EDWARD: *Irish Families, their names, Arms and Origins.* Dublin: Hedges, Figgis, and co., Ltd., 1957.

13.—MATTINGLY, GARRET: *Renaissance Diplomacy.* London: Jonathan Cape, 1955.

14.—MONTAIGNE, MICHEL DE: "Of Cannibals" in *Selected Essays,* ed. Blanchard Bates. New York: Modern Library, 1949.

15.—MORISON, S. E.: *Admiral of the Ocean Sea, a Life of Christopher Columbus.* Boston: Little, Brown, 1942.

16.—PARRY, J. H.: *The Age of Reconnaissance.* London: Weisenfeld and Nicolson, 1963.

17.—PENROSE, BOIS: *Travel and Discovery in the Renaissance.* Cambridge: Harvard University Press, 1963.

18.—SKELTON, R. A.; MARSTON, T. E.; PAINTER, G. D.: *The Vinland Map and Tartar Relation.* New Haven: Yale University Press, 1965.

19.—SOMERVILLE, REAR ADMIRAL BOYLE: *Ocean Passages for the World.* London: Hydrographic Society Department, Admiralty, 1950.

20.—THEVET, ANDRE: *Le Brésil et les Brésiliens.* París: Presses Universitaires, 1953.

21.—VARNHAGEN, FRANCISCO ADOLPHO DE, VISCONDE DE PORTO SEGURO: *Historia Geral do Brasil antes da sua separaçao e independencia de Portugal.* Vol. I. S. Paulo-Cayeiras-Rio: Weiszflog Irmaos, 1935.

22.—WATERS, D. W.: *The Art of Navigation in England in Elizabethan and Early Stuart Times.* New Haven: Yale University Press, 1958.

23.—WINSOR, JUSTIN: *Narrative and Critical History of America by a corps of eminent historical scholars and specialists under the editorship of Justin Winson,* vol. II. *Spanish exploration and settlements on America from the 15th century to the 17th century.* Boston: Houghton Mifflin, 1886.

ARTICLES

1.—COUTINHO, GAGO: "O Descobrimento do Brasil." Lisboa: Sociedade de Geografia, 1947.

2.—TOMKINS, CALVIN: "In The Outlaw Area". New York: The New Yorker, Jan. 8, 1966.